SPECIAL SERIES IN ETHNOMUSICOLOGY: NO. 1

Published for the Society for Ethnomusicology by the Wesleyan University Press, the Special Series contains scholarly studies of larger scope than can ordinarily be carried in the journal of the Society.

ETHNOMUSICOLOGY AND FOLK MUSIC

Ethnomusicology and Folk Music:

AN INTERNATIONAL BIBLIOGRAPHY OF

DISSERTATIONS AND THESES

Compiled and Annotated by

FRANK GILLIS and ALAN P. MERRIAM

Published for the Society for Ethnomusicology

by the

WESLEYAN UNIVERSITY PRESS

MIDDLETOWN, CONNECTICUT

Copyright © 1966 by the Society for Ethnomusicology

Library of Congress Catalog Card Number 66-23459
Manufactured in the United States of America
FIRST EDITION

Contents

Preface

The compilation of this bibliography of dissertations and theses in ethnomusicology and folk music arose from a more limited project undertaken by Alan P. Merriam in 1960; this was "An Annotated Bibliography of Theses and Dissertations in Ethnomusicology and Folk Music Accepted at American Universities," published in the journal ETHNOMUSICOLOGY (January, 1960, Vol. VI, pp. 21-39). Two years later in the same journal, Frank Gillis published a supplement of 197 titles to the original 180 in which he included citations from both American and foreign universities (ETHNOMUSICOLOGY, September, 1962, Vol. VI, pp. 191-214). The amount of valuable material brought to the attention of ethnomusicologists made it seem important to continue the project, and a large number of additional titles has been gathered from a variety of sources and included in the present work, along with the original listings.

It will be evident to the reader that we have cast our net wide to include a considerable variety of topics, all of which, in our opinion, have relevance to ethnomusicology. Thus we include titles from a number of fields in the humanities and social sciences, as well as some from other areas of science. Folk music, jazz, the education of youth and children in non-Western music, the sociology and psychology of music, the computer in music research, and other subjects are given equal consideration with the more traditional spheres of the music of nonliterate and Near and Far Eastern peoples. The bibliography should provide new sources of material for scholars in ethnomusicology and allied fields, as well as for librarians and others seeking citations of ethnomusicologically oriented scholarly papers.

Complete bibliographic information is given regarding the dissertations and theses and an annotation has been added wherever possible. In many instances the titles themselves indicate the subject matter covered in the work cited, and references made to the location of abstracts and summaries and to imprint data for those titles which have been published will be of further assistance. A number of the doctoral dissertations listed here are available through University Microfilms, Inc., Ann Arbor, Michigan; the listing for these includes reference to the annual volume and page number of that firm's *Dissertation Abstracts* (*D.A.*) where an abstract, an order number, and the cost of a microfilm copy of the dissertation will be found. Masters' theses and doctoral dissertations are generally available through Interlibrary Loan from the institutions at which the work was filed. The Index of Institutions included in this work can be used to direct requests to the proper sources.

Far too many individuals and institutions have contributed items and assistance to this project to be noted individually here; we should, however, like to express again our gratitude to all those previously named in our original publications. Among published works, four should be singled out for special mention: Richard Schall's *Verzeichnis deutschsprachiger musikwissenschaftlicher Dissertationen. 1861-1960* (Kassel, Bärenreiter Verlag, 1963); Frederick J. Dockstader, *The American Indian in Graduate Studies* (N. Y., The Museum of the American Indian and the Heye Foundation, 1957); the various issues of *Doctoral Dissertations in Musicology*, by Helen Hewitt, which have appeared separately and with supplements published annually in the fall issue of the *Journal of the American Musicological Society;* and the manuscript bibliography of masters' theses in music gathered by Catharine K. Miller. The present collection of titles would not be nearly so extensive were it not for items culled from these previously compiled lists and included here.

This bibliography, of course, cannot be considered either complete or final, for no such work is ever accomplished. It is our hope that what has been omitted may be included in a future edition of this work.

Indiana University   F.G.
Bloomington, Indiana   A.P.M.

BIBLIOGRAPHY OF DISSERTATIONS
AND THESES

Bibliography of Dissertations and Theses

1. Abd el Hamid Ambar, Mohammed. *Le Problème de l'influence arabe sur les premiers troubadours.* Paris, thèse lettres, 1947.

2. Abert, Hermann. *Die Lehre vom Ethos in der griechischen Musik.* Tübingen (phil.), 1897. *Pub.: Sammlung musikwiss. Arbeiten 2* (Leipzig, Breitkopf & Härtel, 1899). Pp. viii, 168.

3. Ackermann, Elfriede Marie. *"Das Schlaraffenland" in German Literature and Folksong; Social Aspects of an Earthly Paradise with an Inquiry into its History in European Literature.* Chiago, Ph.D. (germ. lang. and lit.), 1944. Pp. 204, litho.

4. Agarkar, A. J. *The Social Background of Physical Education with Special Reference to the Folk-Dances of Maharashtra.* Bombay, Ph.D., 1947. Pp. 290. *Pub.: Folk-Dance of Maharashtra* (Bombay, 1950).

5. Aigen, Bernhard. *Die Geschichte der Musikinstrumente des ägäischen Raumes bis um 700 v. Chr.* Frankfurt a.M. (phil.), 1963.

6. Albertson, Ruthelle Marjorie. *The American Indian and His Song.* Idaho, M.M., 1941. Pp. 50, bibliog., illus., music.
   A musical characterization of the legend of "No Heart." "It is with this thesis that I present the following musical drama based entirely on the true culture of the Indian."

7. Albin, Alexander. *Indigenous Dances of Mexico.* Northwestern U., M.M., 1956. Pp. viii, 77, bibliog., choreog., music.
   Based on original research. Pt. I deals with Yaqui, Tarahumara, seri, Mayo, Cora, Huichole, Tarasco, Nahatl, Otomi, Totonaco, Huaxteco, Chontale, Huave, Tzeltale, Tzoltzile, Tojolabales, Zapotec, Lacandone, and Maya tribes, giving area, instruments, song types, etc. Pt. II is an analysis of six indigenous dances.

8. Alexander, William Peddie. *Hispanic Folk Music in Intercultural Education in New Mexico.* Geo. Peabody, Ed.D. (music), 1961. Pp. 214. D.A. XXII, 3217.
   The first two sections—historical precedents and contemporary reasons for the minority status of the Spanish Americans, and

3

the literary and musical characteristics of Spanish American folksongs and dances—serve as a background and basis for the subsequent chapters.

9. Allen, Dorothy Eastman. *Indian Music of Mexico Up To the Period of the Conquest and the Culture Which Made It What It Was.* So. California, M.M., 1940. Pp. 454, bibliog., glossary, illus., music.

Discusses the background and survivals of Toltec, Aztec and contemporary Mexican Indian music. Includes a comparative chart of musics.

10. Allen, Mary Emma. *A Comparison of Scores Earned by Negro and White Children on Tests of Melodic and Harmonic Sensitivity.* Syracuse U., M.A. (music), 1941. Pp. 106.

11. Allinger, Helen. *The Mozarabic Hymnal and Chant, with Special Emphasis upon the Hymns of Prudentius.* Union Theol. Sem., D.S.M., 1953. Pp. ii, 233, bibliog., photostats of original manuscripts of hymns.

Deals with the origins of Mozarabic liturgy, hymns and chant, the work of Prudentius and texts of his hymns in Mozarabic breviary.

12. Alspach, Addison M. *Tomesha, a Tone Poem.* Iowa, Ph.D. (music comp.), 1933. Pp. 47, music.

Tomesha means "ground afire," the Paiute name of Death Valley. This orchestral composition "follows loosely the form of the legend."

13. Anderson, Arthur James Outram. *Eclipse Rituals and Procedures of North American Indians in Relation to Their Ceremonial Patterns, from the Point of View of Social Psychology.* So. California, Ph.D. (anthro.), 1940.

14. Anderson, Sara May. *Korean Folk Songs.* Eastman, M.M. (music ed.), 1940. Pp. iii, 103, illus., music.

The author divides the work into two parts, the first dealing with the cultural value of folksongs in public school music, and the second dealing with the history and nature of the folksongs. Twelve songs are analyzed for their musical and/or educational value and are given with piano accompaniment in the appendix.

15. Anderson, Warren DeWitt. *Paideia and Ethos in Hellenic Music, with Special Reference to Literary Evidence Regarding the Modes.* Harvard, Ph.D., 1954. Pp. 645, bibliog.

Studies "to determine the views held during the Hellenic period

4

on music as an ethical force . . ." Includes "A Select Glossary of Musical Terms used by Plato" and text of "The Hibeli Musical Papyrus."

16. Ankermann, Bernhard. *Die afrikanischen Musikinstrumente.* Leipzig (phil.), 1901. Pp. xii, 132. *Pub.: Ethnologisches Notziblatt* 3 (Berlin, K. Museum für Völkerkunde, 1903?), pp. 1 ff.

17. Anthony, A. Eugene. *Campaign Songs as a Factor in American Politics.* Pacific, M.A. (hist. and pol. sci.), 1951. Pp. 153.

18. Appleby, David Percy. *A Study of Selected Compositions by Contemporary Brazilian Composers.* Indiana U., Ph.D. (music), 1956. Pp. v, 230, bibliog., 106 music exs.
    Chapter VIII, entitled "Folk Music," gives the historical background of Brazilian folk music; the influence of Indian, Negro, and Portuguese music on the folk music; and the influence of folk music on "serious" music.

19. Arbatsky, Yury. *Das mazedonische Tupanspiel.* Tirana, 1944. *Pub.: Beating the Tupan in the Central Balkans* (Chicago, The Newberry Library, 1953). Pp. vii, 64, bibliog., illus., map, music.

20. Arima, Daigoro. *Japanische Musikgeschichte auf Grund der Quellenkunde.* Vienna (phil.), 1933.

21. Ariumi, K. *The Fundamental Tone System of Japanese Folksongs.* Tokyo U. Arts, 1956.

22. Arlt, Gustave Otto. *Status of Research in Folk Melodies.* Chicago, M.A. (germ. lang. and lit.), 1929. Pp. 38, music.

23. Armour, Eugene. *The Melodic and Rhythmic Characteristics of the Music of the Traditional Ballad Variants Found in the Southern Appalachians.* New York U., Ph.D. (music ed.), 1961. Pp. 178. *D.A.* XXII, 4368.
    187 traditional ballad tunes from Cecil Sharp's *English Folk Songs from the Southern Appalachians* were selected for investigation.

24. Arro, Elmar. *Über das Musikleben in Estland im 19. Jahrhundert.* Vienna (phil.), 1928.

25. Ashton, Dudley. *An Ethnologic Approach to Regional Dance.* Iowa, Ph.D., 1951. Pp. 797.
    Examines dance forms, world-wide. Chapters on "Regional

Dances of the First Americans" and "Indian Influences" (on Latin American dances).

26. Aslanian, Vahe. *A Comparative Analysis of the Sharagan and Folk Song and Their Role in Armenian Culture.* Claremont C., M.A., 1950. Pp. 121, illus., music, tables.

> "The aim . . . is to acquaint the reader with a realm of music which is relatively unknown, and to . . . compare sacred and secular music . . . the writer has limited his research to only a few types of the innumerable folk songs of Armenia and to a few selected hymns of the Gregorian church. . . . Eight hymns called sharagans from the Armenian church music," are also used for comparison.

27. Astraquillo, Corbelita J. *A Study and Evaluation of the Development of Vocal Art Music in the Philippines During the First Half of the Twentieth Century.* Indiana U., Ph.D. (music), 1962. Pp. v, 171, bibliog., music.

> A chapter deals with "The Stylistic Use of the Folk Song in Vocal Literature During the First Half of the Twentieth Century."

28. Ater, Elma Louise. *A Historical Study of the Singing Conventions of the Indians of Robeson County, North Carolina.* Ohio State U., M.A. (music), 1943.

29. Au, Hans von der. *Das Volkstanzgut im Rheinfränkischen.* Giessen (phil.), 1939. Pub.: *Giessener Beitr. z. dt. Philologie* 70 (Giessen, von Münchow, 1939). Pp. 157.

30. Aycock, Etholine Grigsby. *Americanisms in the Traditional Ballads of the Eastern United States.* Missouri, M.A. (engl.), 1940.

31. Ayyangar, Ranganayaki. *Analysis of the Melodic, Rhythmic and Formal Structure of Karnātic Kriti as Exemplified in the Kritis of Śrī Śyāma Śāstrī, Śrī Muttusvāmī Dīkṣitar and Śrī Tyāgarāja.* Hawaii, M.A. (music), 1965. Pp. vi, 305, bibliog., 145 pp. music, 10 tables, 27 pp. texts in Devanāgari, transliteration and translation, glossary. A tape recording, 30′ 25″, is deposited separately.

> The study includes a review of the historical background of this South Indian vocal genre, seven representative selections as sung by the author (a soloist of All India Radio) in a double transcription (one prescriptive in intent, being a direct transcription of the Karnātic solmization with ornament symbols; the other

descriptive of the given recorded performance with a relatively high level of specificity of detail), and analysis of the musical content.

32. Bailey, Frederick. *The Historical Ballad: Its Tradition in Britain and America*. Tennessee, Ph.D. (folkl.), 1963. Pp. 198. *D.A.* XXV, 395.

   A study based on ballads showing signs of traditional life as gathered from Child's *English and Scottish Popular Ballads* and from collections of British and American balladry since Child. It is shown that ballads are not a trustworthy guide to history.

33. Bailey, Virginia May. *An Evaluation of the Musical Expression of the Southern California Indians*. Claremont C., M.A., 1934. Pp. 91, music.

   From the viewpoints of the values to be gained in the study of the development of music, archaeological aspects, sociological aspects, and historical aspects.

34. Bakărdžiev, Georgi N. *Untersuchungen zur melodischen Gestalt des bulgarischen Volksliedes*. Prague (phil.), 1940-42. Pp. 103.

35. Baker, Richard Gene. *The Changing Philosophies Found in Twentieth Century Mexico Concerning Nationalistic Music*. So. California, M.M., 1956. Pp. 345, illus., music.

   Discusses major composers and their approaches to using Indian or Hispanic elements in their music.

36. Baker, Sibyl Evans. *Native Cuban Music: Its Sources and Characteristics*. Northwestern U., M.M., 1937. Pp. 41, bibliog., illus., 19 music exs.

   Contains brief sections on sources of present-day Cuban music; Cuban musical instruments; dance forms; characteristic elements of Cuban music.

37. Bane, Mildred E. *The American Folksong in Music Education*. Illinois Wesleyan U., M.A. (music), 1945.

38. Banyay, I. K. *The History of the Hungarian Music*. So. California, M.M., 1942. Pp. 893, music.

   Primarily a history of art and religious music, the thesis includes a chapter on Gypsy music and one on the instruments of the Magyars.

39. Barkechli, Mehdi. *La Gamme de la musique iranienne*. Paris, thèse de sciences, 1948. *Pub.*: included in the author's *Musique traditionelle de l'Iran* ... (Teheran, 1964).

7

40. Barksdale, Rubie Jeanni. *Social, Religious and Economic Influences on the Origin of Dance.* Geo. Peabody, M.A. (phy. ed.), 1930. Pp. 130.

41. Barnard, Herwanna Becker. *The Comanche and His Literature with an Anthology of His Myths, Legends, Folktales, Oratory, Poetry, and Songs.* Oklahoma, M.A., 1941. Pp. vi, 277.
    The study is divided into two parts: the first, the general information necessary to understand the Comanche; the second, the myths, legends, folktales, oratory, poetry and songs that have been collected, classified, and annotated. No music notations; song texts are given.

42. Barrelet, Mina. *Mallorkinische Volkslieder und Tänze gesammelt von M. Antoni Jusep Pont (mallorkin. Geistl.), hrsg. u. erläut.* Hamburg (phil.), 1923. Pp. vi, 221, 47.

43. Baskerville, David. *The Interplay of Jazz and Serious Music in the 1920's.* California (Los Angeles), Ph. D. In process.

44. Bateman, Ruby Gleanes. *The Mask and Its Significance in the Dance.* Geo. Peabody, M.A. (phy. ed.), 1936. Pp. 161.

45. Baxter, Glen William. *Hua-Chien Chi: Songs of Tenth-Century China. A Study of the First Tz'u Anthology.* Harvard, Ph.D., 1952. Pp. 317. Descriptive bibliography of editions; texts and transliteration of 60 *tz'u* (representing all 18 poets); index to *Ch'in ting tz'u catalogue.* *Pub.*: Cambridge, Mass., Harvard-Yenching Institute, 1951. Mimeo.

46. Beck, Horace Palmer, Jr. *Down-East Ballads and Songs.* Pennsylvania, Ph.D. (lang. and lit.), 1952. Pp. 433. *D.A.* XII, 293.
    120 songs collected in Maine dealing with songs sung around the home, in the logging camps and aboard ship. Includes discussions of each category before listing the songs chronologically, with notes explaining and discussing aspects of the song hitherto unnoted, and a selective bibliography. A section deals with miscellany, including bawdy songs.

47. Becker, Babette Minnie. *Music in the Life of Ancient China as Reflected in the Ceremonial Books: The I li, the Chou li, the Li chi.* Chicago, M.A. (oriental lang. and lit.), 1954. Pp. 39, bibliog.
    From the records in the ceremonial books, aspects of which are described in detail, this study shows that "music was an indispensable element of personal and social life in early China and a significant subject of philosophic speculation."

8

48. Becker, Babette Minnie. *Music in the Life of Ancient China: From 1400 B.C. to 300 B.C.* Chicago, Ph.D. (oriental lang. and lit.), 1957. Pp. 98, bibliog.

   The five chapters deal with oracle bones and bronze inscriptions; the *I Ching* and the *Shu Ching;* music in the *Shih Ching;* Confucius and music; Mo Tzu and music; Mencius and music.

49. Becker, Howard Saul. *The Professional Dance Musician in Chicago.* Chicago, A.M. (sociol.), 1949. Pp. 140, bibliog., illus.

   Based on interviews with over 100 musicians and on observational data, the study deals with two problems: how dance musicians as a group organize to meet the constant need for jobs; their feelings about their roles in relation to non-musicians. Chapters include the dance orchestra, the informal organization of the profession, the musician and the businessman, the musician and his audience, the musician and the union, the career of the dance musician.

50. Beckwith, Martha Warren. *Dance Forms of the Moqui and Kwakiutl Indians.* Columbia U., M.A., 1906. Pp. 43. *Pub.:* 15th Intl. Cong. Americanists, *Proc.,* pt. 2 (1907).

51. Belton, Geneva R. *The Contributions of Negro Music and Musicians in World War II.* Northwestern U., M.M. (music), 1946. Pp. 64.

52. Benedict, Laura E. W. *A Study of Bagobo Ceremonial, Magic, and Myth.* Columbia U., Ph. D. (anthro.), 1914. Pp. 307, bibliog., illus., index, vita.

   Describes Bagobo mythological concepts, seven formal rites in detail, chant, agong music, texts of antiphonal chants, daily forms of religious response, sources of myth.

53. Benner, Blair Mitchell. *Instruments of the Belgian Congo.* Boston U., M.A., 1949. Pp. 147, bibliog., illus., map, plates.

   Introduction includes a brief history of the tribes of the region, ethnological procedures involved, and correlations. Sources include monographs, critical papers, and material given the author by missionaries to the Congo. Discussion includes idiophones, membranophones, chordophones, and aerophones.

54. Bennet, David Parker. *A Study of Fiddle Tunes from Western North Carolina.* North Carolina, M.A. (music), 1940. Pp. 90.

55. Bennett, John Paul. *Music in the Coptic Church of Egypt and Ethiopia.* Washington, M.A. (music ed.), 1945. Pp. iii, 85, bibliog.

   A history of the Coptic Church and its liturgical system. Also a description of the musical system, including instruments, notation, modes, and a comparison with Gregorian Chant.

56. Bergsagel, John Dagfinn. *The National Aspects of the Music of Ralph Vaughan Williams.* Cornell U., Ph.D. (music), 1957. Pp. 329, bibliog. *D.A.* XVII, 2026.

Chapters are devoted to investigations on the nature and influence of English folksong and of English Tudor music on Vaughn Williams' musical style.

57. Berner, Alfred. *Studien zur arabischen Musik auf Grund der gegenwärtigen Theorie und Praxis in Ägypten. Berlin* (phil.), 1937. *Pub.*: Bottrop, W. Postberg, 1937. Also: *Schriftenreihe des Staatlichen Instituts für deutsche Musikforschung,* Heft 2 (Leipzig, Kistner & Siegel, 1937). Pp. vi, 124. Review in *Archiv für Musikforschung* 3 (1938), pp. 123-26.

58. Bernoulli, Eduard. *Aus Liederbüchern der Humanistenzeit. Eine bibliographische und notentypographische Studie.* Zürich (HabSchr.), 1910. *Pub.*: Leipzig, Breitkopf & Härtel, 1910. Pp. 116.

59. Betterton, William Fred. *A History of Music in Davenport, Iowa, Before 1900.* Iowa, Ph.D. (music ed.), 1962. Pp. 707. *D.A.* XXIII, 2933.

All aspects of the music of this city, especially influences brought in by the German immigrants of 1848, are discussed.

60. Billups, Kenneth Brown. *The Inclusion of Negro Music as a Course of Study in the School Curriculum.* Northwestern U., M.M., 1947.

61. Bingham, Carl W. *A Comparison of Certain Phases of Musical Ability of Negro and White Public School Pupils.* Texas, M.A., 1925.

62. Black, Robert A. *A Content Analysis of 81 Hopi Chants.* Indiana U., Ph.D. (anthro.), 1964. Pp. xli, 456, bibliog., 26 tables, no music.

Treats secular chants, or announcement-making (referred to as crying (criers) in the literature). The chant variations studied were selected from a corpus representing 11 genres of subject matter and were gathered during the summers of 1957, 1958 and 1960 on the Hopi Indian Reservation in northern Arizona.

63. Blacking, John. *The Cultural Foundations of the Music of the Venda, with Special Reference to Their Children's Songs.* Witwatersrand, Ph.D., 1964. Pp. xxiv, 486, bibliog., map, music, photos, tables.

Part I, consisting of two chapters, deals with definitions and concepts of music and dancing, music instruments, performance, form and meaning, development of musical talent, and musical taste. A second part, chapters 3 through 7, includes a cultural, musical and textual analysis of 56 children's songs. Part III has three chapters treating "Cultural Patterns and Musical Form," "Musical Expression as a Function of Cultural Background" and "Problems of Method in Cultural Analyses of Music."

64. Blair, Leola Ruth. *A Study of the Cultural Heritage of the California Children from the Indians.* So. California, M.M., 1947. Pp. 154, bibliog., illus., music.

Describes music and dance of each tribe. Includes a list of recordings in the Museum of the University of California at Berkeley. Not based on original field research.

65. Bluestein, Eugene. *The Background and Sources of an American Folksong Tradition.* Minnesota, Ph.D. (american studies), 1960. Pp. vii, 200, bibliog.

"An historical study of the assumptions and preconceptions upon which folklorists in the nineteenth and twentieth centuries based their estimates of the origins and nature of American folksong traditions." Herder, Emerson, Whitman, the Lomaxes, the Child ballad tradition and the Negro are discussed.

66. Blum, Fred. *Susanne Langer's Music Aesthetics.* Iowa, Ph.D. (musicol.), 1959. Pp. xxv, 435. *D.A.* XX, 1037.

Early chapters examine Dr. Langer's philosophical premises for her aesthetics in general and her music aesthetics in particular, and expound and criticize her notions of music's semblance, symbol and import in the light of her premises. Later chapters deal with the distinctions between the musical symbol and the symbol in music, with the relations among the arts, and with the implications of Langer's teleological premise for her theory of the origin and history of music.

67. Bock, Betty. *Broadcast Songs; a Paradox in Monopoly Control.* Bryn Mawr C., Ph.D. (econ.), 1942. Pp. 97. *D.A.* VII, no. 1, pp. 17-19.

Considers the legal and economic issues concerned with the popular song composer, ASCAP and BMI, and the radio broadcasting industry.

68. Boehm, Beat. *Heilende Musik im griechischen Altertum.* Basel (med.), 1958. *Pub.: Zeitschr. für Psychotherapie u. med. Psychologie* 8 (1958), part 4, pp. 132-151.

69. Böhm, Max. *Volkslied, Volkstanz und Kinderlied in Mainfranken. Ein Beitrag zur Erforschung fränkischer Melodien (unter Beziehung auf das Volkslied der Rheinpfalz).* Erlangen (phil.), 1928 (1929). *Pub.:* Nuremberg, Zorn, 1929. Pp. vi, 256.

70. Bogan, Phebe M. *The Ceremonial Dances of the Yaqui Indians near Tucson, Arizona.* Arizona, M.A. (hist.), 1922. Pp. 87. *Pub.:* under title *Yaqui Indian Dances of Tucson, Arizona.* Tucson, Arizona, The Archeol. Soc., 1925. Pp. 69, illus.
    An account of the drama and accompanying dances of the Lenten season at Pascua village. There is no consideration of the music.

71. Bonar, Eleanor Jean. *A Collection of Ballads and Popular Songs, Iowa and Appalachian.* Iowa, M.A. (engl.), 1930. Pp. ii, 224.
    104 songs collected by the author and others in Iowa and Kentucky, many without music. The author attempted to include principally songs unpublished or found only in obscure publications.

72. Borga, Horatiu D. *Les Chants funèbres chez les peuples du Bas-Danube. Etude descriptive de folklore albanais, bulgare, roumain et serbe.* Strasbourg, thèse lettres, 1954. Pp. 370.

73. Borgman, George Allan. *Nationalism in Contemporary American Music.* Indiana U., M.M., 1953. Pp. iv, 83, bibliog., music, tables.
    Discusses the jazz idiom, traditional tunes, dance, cowboy, Indian elements, spirituals.

74. Borthwick, E. K. *The Influence of Music on Greek Life and Thought.* Cambridge (C.C.), Ph.D. (anc. hist.), 1952.

75. Bose, Fritz. *Die Musik der Uitoto.* Berlin (phil.), 1934. Pp. 40, 19, iv. *Pub.: Zeitschr. f. vgl. Musikwiss.* 2 (1934).

76. Boswell, George W. *Reciprocal Influences of Text and Tune in the Southern Traditional Ballad.* Geo. Peabody, Ph.D. (engl. lit.), 1951. Pp. 209. *Pub.: Peabody Contribs. to Educ.,* no. 434.

77. Botkin, Benjamin Albert. *The American Play-Party Song; With a Collection of Oklahoma Texts and Tunes.* Nebraska, Ph.D., 1931. *Pub.*: Univ. of Neb., *University Studies*, XXXVII, nos. 1-4 (1937). Pp. 400, bibliog., indexes, map, music.
    Over 1000 variants of 128 songs, representative of the play-party usage of both the younger and older generations of Oklahoma, collected by teachers, students and other interested individuals. Part 1: discussion of origins and backgrounds, the play-party and the game, the dance and the song, and language and style; Part II: texts and tunes.

78. Botte, Marie D. *Selections of Tunes and Variations in the Words of Certain Folk Tunes and Ballads of the Upper Monongahela Valley.* Ohio U., M.A. (music), 1942.

79. Bouillon, Elisabeth. *Zum Verhältnis von Text und Melodie in den schottisch-englischen Volksballaden.* Bonn (phil.), 1960.

80. Boynton, John Henry. *Studies in the English Ballad Refrain With a Collection of Ballad and Early Song Refrains.* Harvard, Ph.D., 1897. 3 vols. Pp. 619, bibliog., tables.

81. Boyter, Haskell L. *The Status of Public School Music Among Negroes in the State of Georgia.* Eastman, M.M., 1944.

82. Brandel, Rose. *The Music of Central Africa—an Ethnomusicological Study—French Equatorial Africa, the Belgian Congo and Ruanda-Urundi, Uganda, Tanganyika.* New York U., Ph.D. (music), 1959. Vol. I: pp. 231, discussion of culture, ritual, music, including dance and musical instruments; Vol. II: pp. 139, transcriptions and charts. *Pub.*: The Hague, M. Nijhoff, 1961. Pp. xii, 272.

83. Braschowanoff, Stojern. *Über die Rhythmik und Metrik des bulgarischen Volksliedes.* Leipzig (phil.), 1923. Pp. 32. Summary in *Jahrb. d. phil. Fak. Leipzig*, 1923, part 1, pp. 80-81.

84. Braune, Gerd. *Der Einfluss von Schallplatte und Rundfunk auf die deutsche Musikinstrumentenindustrie.* Nuremberg (Handelshochschule), 1934 (1933). Pp. 146.

85. Breloer, Bernhard. *Die Grundelemente der altindischen Musik nach dem Bhāaratiya-nātya-śāstra. Text, Übersetzung und Erklärung.* Bonn (phil.), 1922. Pp. 48.

86. Brennan, Mary Ellen. *The Material Used in Ancient Modes: Greek and Ecclesiastical.* Northwestern U., M.M., 1947.

87. Brewster, Paul G. *Ballads and Songs of Indiana.* Indiana U., Ph.D., 1940. *Pub.*: Indiana Univ., *Pubs.*, Folklore Series 1 (Bloomington, 1940). Pp. 376, bibliog., indexes, music.
    Author presents 100 ballads and songs, many of them with two or more variants. Brief history, bibliography and texts for each ballad and song. Twenty-seven are Child ballads and about thirty include simple tunes.

88. Bringemeier, Martha. *Gemeinschaft und Volkslied.* Münster (phil.), 1931. *Pub.*: *Veröff. d. volksk. Komm. d. Provinzialinst. f. westf. Landesu.* Volkskunde 1 (Münster i.W., Aschendorff, 1931). Pp. 256.

89. Britton, Allen Perdue. *Theoretical Introductions in American Tune-Books to 1800.* Michigan, Ph.D. (music), 1950. Pp. 697, bibliog. *D.A.* X, 97.
    Part I: origin and musical implications of Protestant psalmody, the advent of vocal music instruction in the American Colonies, and the general output of tune-books during the eighteenth century; Part II: annotated bibliography of tune-books, giving location of each work cited. Includes other bibliographies.

90. Brömse, Peter. *Flöten, Schalmeien und Sackpfeifen Südslawiens.* Prague (phil.), 1935. *Pub.*: *Veröff. des musikwiss. Institutes der Deutschen Universität in Prag.* 9 (Brünn, Rohrer, 1937). Pp. 110.

91. Broucek, Jack Wolf. *Eighteenth Century Music in Savannah, Georgia.* Florida State U., Ed.D. (music ed.), 1963. Pp. 256. *D.A.* XXIV, 321.
    A chapter indicates the contributions to the city's musical conditions by such religious and nationalistic groups as the Moravians, Salzburgers, Negroes, Indians, Scots, Spaniards and Jews.

92. Brough, Rosemary Joy. *Lucky, the Opportunist; A Psychobiological Personality Study of a Navaho Singer.* Cornell U., M.A., 1953. Pp. 158.

93. Brouwer, Cornelis. *Das Volkslied in Deutschland, Frankreich, Belgien und Holland.* Groningen (phil.), 1930. *Pub.*: Groningen, Wolter, 1930. Pp. 251.

94. Brown, Anita. *Étude de la chanson populaire de la France au point de vue poetique.* So. California, M.A., 1912. Pp. 50, bibliog.

> Selections of popular songs from the seventeenth to nineteenth centuries with annotations.

95. Brown, Donald N. *The Dance of Taos Pueblo.* Harvard (Senior Honors Thesis), 1959.

96. Brown, Dorothy Oshern. *Civil War Songs in the Harris Collection of American Poetry at Brown University.* Brown U., M.A. (music and educ.), 1959. Pp. 192, bibliog.

> Gives the following for each entry: title, composer, author, publisher, date, key signature, meter, form.

97. Brown, G. Boylston. *A Survey of Iberian Folk-Song and a Study of the Jota Aragonesa.* Eastman, M.A. (musicol.), 1935. Pp. iv, 170, illus., music.

> After giving a short history of Iberian folksong, the author analyzes the *jota aragonesa* from the point of view of rhythm, modality, accompaniment, melody, words, and the dance.

98. Brown, Ray B. *Alabama Folk Songs.* California (Los Angeles), Ph.D. (engl.), 1956. Pp. 625, bibliog., music.

> 201 songs, most with music, and many appearing for the first time in any collection. Categorized into nine sections: love song-courting (89 examples); happy love songs (37); unhappy love songs (23); anti-marriage (8); comical love (14); sentimental (12); social commentary (6); satiric (7); parodies of songs (5). Index by title, first line, and refrain.

99. Browne, Earl William. *Variant Versions of Scottish and English Humorous Popular Ballads in America.* So. California, A.M. (engl.), 1951. Pp. 343, map.

> Study of text variations in "The Farmer's Curst Wife," "Our Goodman," "Get Up and Bar the Door," and "The Wife Wrapt in Wether's Skin."

100. Browne, Earl William. *Variant Forms of English and Scottish Popular Ballads in America.* California (Los Angeles), Ph.D. (lang. and lit.), 1961.

101. Bruinsma, Henry Allen. *The Souterliedekens and Its Relation to Psalmody in the Netherlands.* Michigan, Ph.D., 1949. *D.A.* IX, 148.

> "The *Souterliedekens* is a collection of psalm translations set to folk tunes which was printed in the Netherlands in a small

volume in 1540. It was the first metrical translation of the psalms into the vernacular and as a collection of printed folk music provides us with the most complete reference work of sixteenth-century Dutch folk tunes."

102. Brunner-Traut, Emma. *Der Tanz im alten Ägypten. Nach bildlichen und inschriftlichen Zeugnissen.* Munich (phil.), 1937 (1938). *Pub.: Ägyptologische Forschungen* 6 (Glükstadt, Augustin, 1938). Pp. 91.

103. Bruno, James Byron. *Folk Music Materials for Use in the Elementary School.* New York U., Ed.D. (music), 1960. 2 vols. Pp. 270. *D.A. XXI*, 3112.
   "The research uncovered a strong consensus concerning the particular appropriateness of folk music for this purpose, not only because it high-lights the background and customs of other nationalities and geographical locations, but also because of its earthy character, its simplicity and its common appeal as an expression of the people." Material listed includes folksongs, folk dances, and recorded folk music, giving such information as title, origin and comments for each entry.

104. Buchheim, Lotte. *Volksliedhaftes unter Büchers deutschen Arbeitsliedern. Eine Untersuchung an Hand der deutschen Arbeitslieder in Karl Büchers "Arbeit und Rhythmus."* Leipzig (phil.), 1931. Pp. 113.

105. Buckley, Bruce Redfern. *Frankie and Her Men: A Study of the Interrelationships of Popular and Folk Traditions.* Indiana U., Ph.D. (folkl.), 1962. Pp. 297. *D.A. XXIII*, 2484.
   An examination of the ballad "Frankie and Albert" (Laws 1-3), in which the major content elements were traced in 291 versions showing the various stages of change in the folk versions as popular versions were introduced.

106. Beuschel, Gordon Richard. *Indian Song and Dance.* Northwestern U., M.M., 1948. Pp. 63, bibliog., music.
   Presentation, transcription and analysis of ten Ogallala Sioux songs not hitherto published; description of ten dances, unspecified as to tribe but apparently Plains. Very brief and general description of music in Indian life.

107. Buford, Mary Elizabeth. *Folk Songs of Florida and Texas.* So. Methodist U., M.A. (engl.), 1941. Pp. 219.

108. Burger, Erich. *Deutsche Kirchenmelodien in Schweden. Ein Beitrag zur Geschichte der schwedischen Reformation.* Munich (phil.), 1933. *Pub.: Kyrkohistorisk Årsskrift*, 1932, pp. 108-271.

16

109. Burnett, Madeline Land. *The Development of American Hymnody, 1620-1900.* So. California, M.A. (music), 1946. Pp. 112.

110. Burns, Betty. *The Function of Music in the Inca Society.* Northwestern U., M.M., 1954. Pp. x, 219, bibliog., 40 figs., 51 music exs.
> Contains chapters on historical background, Inca culture, musical instruments, the function of music in Inca society, contemporary use of Inca music.

111. Bussfeld, Bernhard. *Die polymetrischen Chorlieder in Senecas Oedipus und Agamemnon.* Münster (phil.), 1935. *Pub.:* Bochum, Pöpinghaus, 1935. Pp. ii, 63.

112. Cady, Carolyn P. *Some Aspects of Native Cuban Music.* Columbia U., M.A. (music), 1932. Pp. 93, bibliog., music exs.
> A survey of the topic, manners of performance, and content of the music with twenty pages of examples.

113. Caldwell, George O. *A Comparison of Selected Material in Stravinsky's "Fire Bird" with Traditional Negro Folk Music.* Iowa, M.A. (music), 1932.

114. Calhoun, Cecil Warner. *Selected Instrumental Folk Music of South Central Kentucky.* Iowa, M.A. (music), 1941. Pp. iii, 88.
> Study and 53 tunes. The author, a native of the region and from a family of folk musicians, gathered the material from his own circle.

115. Camp, Charles MacLeod. *The Musical Bow in Southern Africa.* Indiana U., A.M. (anthro.), 1953. Pp. iii, 51, bibliog., 2 drawings, 2 maps, 2 photos, 1 table.
> Deals with the typology, distribution, manner of playing, musical style, and cultural aspects of the musical bow.

116. Candor, Ethel. *The Musical Talent of Mexican School Children.* Denver, M.A. (educ. and psychol.), 1933. Pp. 39, bibliog.
> An experimental study of the musical talent of 700 school children of Mexico City by means of the *Measures of Musical Talent,* by Carl E. Seashore. Conclusion: no real racial differences exist.

117. Carpenter, James Madison. *Forecastle Songs and Chanties.* Harvard, Ph.D., 1929. Pp. 564, bibliog.
> Texts, with commentary, to many sea songs taken mostly from location interviews.

118. Carpenter, Rosa Lillian. *The Use of Negro Music in Negro Schools.* Northwestern U., M.M., 1940.

119. Carrel, Anna J. *The Gypsy Trail Through Music.* Cincinnati Conserv. of Music, M.M., 1937.

120. Carruth, Wincie Ann. *The Significance of Religion in the Dance.* Louisiana State U., M.A. (phy. ed.), 1937. Pp. 94.

121. Carter, Albert E. *The Louisiana Negro and His Music.* Northwestern U., M.M., 1947. Pp. ii, 68, bibliog., music.
    The purpose of the study is to show the Louisiana Negro's contribution to American music, particularly folk music; included are chapters on Africa, occupational songs, blues and hollers, swing, Creole songs, and spirituals. From first-hand experience on the part of the author, a native of Louisiana.

122. Cason, Georgie Rees. *An Introduction to a Study of California Indian Music.* California (Berkeley), M.A. (music), 1937. Pp. 70, bibliog., illus., music.
    The thesis covers three aspects of California Indian music: 1) tabulation of references to music in religious ceremonies, origin myths, etc.; 2) listing of instruments used in the area; 3) song analysis, using material from previously collected sources. The instrumental section, which deals with material not published in other sources, is most valuable, and is accompanied by black and white sketches.

123. Castren, David Charles. *Philosophical and Historical Observations Concerning Chinese Musical Phenomena.* Minnesota, M.A. (music), 1959. Pp. 52, text; pp. 38, bibliog. and tables.
    The author utilized philosophic, historic and ethnic writings of the ancient Chinese, as well as musical sources, in his observations on the dualism of the "Yin" and "Yang"; the origin of the music pitch-pipes or *"lüs"*; the legend concerning the "Yellow Emperor" and his Music Ruler; and the "number" system in the Chinese civilization. A chapter is devoted to a "look at the ancient Greek philosophers and their influence upon the Western world, specifically music where a striking parallel between East and West emerged."

124. Cavallo, J. R. *Kumanche of the Zuni Indians.* Wesleyan U., B.A. (Distinction Thesis), 1956. Pp. iv, 110, illus., music, tables.
    A study of the meaning and place of Kumanche among the sacred dances of the Zuni Indians. The thesis includes costume drawings, a glossary of Zuni words, and music of many of the songs.

18

125. Chamberlain, William W. *Folk Music in the Kentucky Barrens.* Stanford U., M.A. (engl.), 1940. Pp. 239.

126. Chapman, A. D. *English Folk-Carols and the Dance.* McGill U., M.A., 1937.

127. Charles, Norman. *Social Values in American Popular Songs (1890-1950).* Pennsylvania, Ph.D. (hist.), 1958. Pp. 249. D.A. XIX, 783.
    Attempts "to establish that the verbal content of popular songs . . . reveals significant variations from year to year, and that these variations point to shifts in the national state of mind." The denotative content of more than 1000 popular songs is classified.

128. Chastain, Regina Carey. *Spanish Influences on Mexican Music.* Boston U., M.A., 1945. Pp. [4] ii, 73, bibliog., music.

129. Chesarek, Eleanor. *A Study of Slovenia and Its Folk Music with Representative Selections Suitable for Use in American Schools.* So. California, M.M., 1949. Pp. 164, music.
    Music of Slovenia, based on English sources and Yugoslav music collections.

130. Chesky, Jane. *The Nature and Function of Papago Music.* Arizona, M.A., 1943. Pp. 137, music.
    From a study of several months conducted at Gu Achi, the writer finds much aboriginal Papago music survives and that European music is also used for religious and social occasions. Songs are transcribed and the melodic and rhythmic patterns analyzed.

131. Chrisman, Katharine Vada. *A Study of Pre-Classic Dance Forms.* Geo. Peabody, M.A. (phy. ed.), 1937. Pp. 118.

132. Christensen, Dieter. *Die Musik der Kate und Sialum: Beiträge zur Ethnographie Neuguineas.* Berlin, F.U. (phil.), 1957. Pp. 126, music, tables. *Pub.*: Berlin, author, 1957. Pp. 127, map, music, tables, vita.
    Based on 49 Edison cylinders made in New Guinea by Richard Neuhauss in 1908-1910 and now housed in the Berlin Phonogrammarchiv. Considers cultural background as well as style, presents descriptive and tabular analyses, and gives transcriptions of 52 songs.

133. Christensen, Vivian Marquis. *Development of South American Music.* Northwestern U., M.M., 1940.

134. Clausen, Raymond E. *A Musicological Study of the Layard Collection of Recorded Malekulan Music in Its Sociological and Ritual Setting.* Oxford (Exeter), B. Litt., 1958.

135. Clifford, Barbara Marr. *"Hiawatha, an Indian Boy": An Operetta Based on Henry W. Longfellow's Poem.* New York U., Ed.D., 1941. Pp. 104, music.
    An operetta for children. It is not known to what extent Indian musical themes are used.

136. Clive, Joseph C. *Music of the Pahute Indians.* Utah, M.S. (music), 1949. Pp. xi, 44, incl. 23 music exs., which are paginated, 21 recordings.
    Based on research among the "Pahute" of southern Utah (reservation not stated), taken from informants in Cedar City and Blanding, Utah. Musical transcriptions of 21 songs, no texts; analysis along Western harmonic lines.

137. Coffin, Tristram P. *A Handbook of the Traditional Ballad in North America.* Pennsylvania, Ph.D. (engl. lit.), 1949. *Pub.*: Amer. Folklore Soc., *Pubs.*, Bibl. Ser., vol. 2 (Philadelphia, 1950). Pp. xvi, 188, bibliog., indexes, no music.
    A critical, bibliographical study of the Child ballads and their variants.

138. Cohen, Ethel S. *The Wedding Songs of the Babylonian Jews.* New York U., M.A. (music), 1940.

139. Coine, Harriett Edythe. *The Play Life of Certain Indian Tribes in California.* So. California, M.A., 1932. Pp. 65, bibliog., diagrs.
    Includes their dances through which "they give expression to aesthetic and moral attitudes."

140. Coker, Jerry. *An Introduction to the Theory of Jazz Improvisation.* Sam Houston S.T.C., M.A. (music ed.), 1960. Pp. 99, bibliog., charts, diagrs., music, tables. *Pub.*: under the title *Improvising Jazz* (Englewood Cliffs, New Jersey, Prentice-Hall, 1964; paperbound). Pp. xii, 115.
    Presents the theoretical principles used in jazz as they apply to the ultimate improvised performance. Chapters include discussions on melody, the rhythm section, chord types and superimposition, and the development of the ear. Appendix A deals with the "Aesthetic Criteria for the Evaluation of a Jazz Artist"; Appendix B, "Some Possibilities for Voicings"; and C and D contain close to 100 characteristic chord progressions.

141. Combs, Josiah Henry. *Folk-Songs du midi des États-Unis*. Paris, Lett. D., 1925. *Pub.*: Paris, Les Presses Universitaires de France, 1925. Pp. 230.

> Part I: "Folk-Songs du midi des États-Unis"; Part 2: texts to 25 "Chansons d'origine anglaise" (pp. 127-176) and texts to 34 "Chanson indigènes d'Amerique" (pp. 176-227). Bibliography at end of each chapter. Songs and ballads (some Child variants) collected in Kentucky, Virginia, West Virginia, Tennessee, Arkansas, Oklahoma, and Texas, 1910-25.

142. Connick, Roxane. *A Survey of South African Native Music*. New York U., M.A. (music), 1949. Pp. 106, bibliog., 3 charts, illus., music.

> Summarizes the historical references of early travelers on South African music, and all work by modern scholars. Organizes the materials in terms of the three main cultural groups of African peoples.

143. Cook, Harold. *Shaker Music: A Manifestation of American Folk Culture*. Western Reserve U., Ph.D. (music), 1947. Pp. 301.

144. Cooke, Frederick A. P. *American Indian Music and Dancing*. Coll. of Music of Cincinnati, M.M., 1934.

145. Cooper, Jane. *Characteristics of American Folk Music*. College-Conserv. of Music of Cincinnati, M.M., 1951. Pp. 68, bibliog., music.

> Discussion of definition, characteristics, and future of folk music in America, including Negro and American Indian examples.

146. Cornwell, Elizabeth. *Regional Variations in the Characteristics of American Square, Contra and Round Dances in Certain Regions of the United States*. Wellesley C., M.S. (phy. ed.), 1943. Pp. 101.

147. Costa, Mazeppa King. *Dance in the Society and Hawaiian Islands as Presented by the Early Writers, 1767-1842*. Hawaii, M.A. (drama), 1951. Pp. 151.

> The first section is a compilation of references to dance in the islands as recorded by the earliest European observers, before European acculturation took place. The second part attempts an analysis of the dances, modeled on classifications as given in Curt Sachs' *World History of the Dance*.

148. Covell, Frank Jack. *The National Hymns of the Spanish-American Republics*. Stanford U., M.A. (rom. langs.), 1940. Pp. 81.

149. Covington, Louise Donaldson. *The Religious Dance of Ancient Civilizations and Its Modern Revival.* Geo. Peabody, M.A. (phy. ed.), 1936. Pp. 66.

150. Cowan, Clayton Leroy. *Irish Folksong Elements in American Popular Music.* So. California, M.A. (music), 1950. Pp. 125, music.
    Covers American popular music from 1860 to 1900. Shows emotional rather than musical connections between true Irish music and American-Irish tunes.

151. Cox, John Harrington. *The Ballads and Songs of West Virginia.* Harvard, Ph.D., 1923. Pp. xxxiv, 711, music. *Pub.*: Wash., D.C., National Service Bureau. American Folk-Song Publications, No. 3 and No. 5 (1939). Also, *Folk-Songs of the South* (Cambridge, Mass., Harvard Univ. Press, 1925).
    About 190 folksong texts, with melody inserted from time to time, collected and edited by the author from various informants.

152. Craig, Grace L. *Communal Composition of Ballads: A Comparative Study of Finnish, Russian and Czechoslovakian Ballads, Collected by the Writer.* McGill U., M.A., 1934.

153. Crawford, Lucille Hayes. *The Musical Activities of James Weldon Johnson.* Fisk U., M.A. (music), 1941. Pp. 56.

154. Creed, Ruth. *African Influence on Latin American Music.* Northwestern U., M.M., 1947. Pp. 106, bibliog., illus., maps, 28 music exs.
    Short chapters on Cuba, Puerto Rico, Dominican Republic, Martinique, Jamaica, Trinidad, Haiti, Dutch Guiana, Brazil, with examples of each drawn from previously published sources.

155. Crews, Emma Katherine. *A History of Music in Knoxville, Tennessee, 1791 to 1910.* Florida State U., Ed.D. (music), 1961. Pp. 253. *D.A.* XXII, 2815.
    Considers dance music, music for celebrations.

156. Crossman, Max William. *Bibliographical Materials for the Study of Folk Music in the U.S.* Michigan, M.A. (music), 1946. Pp. 45.

157. Crowle, Hazel Araminta. *An Interpretive Study of the Official Jarabe Tapatio, the National Dance of Old Mexico.* San Jose S.C., M.A., 1952. Pp. 114.

158. Crutchfield, Mary Elizabeth. *The White Spiritual.* Union Theol. Sem., M.A. (music), 1946.

159. Cullins, Ella Webb. *Origin of American Negro Folkways.* Boston U., M.A., 1942. Pp. 83, music, tables.
> The purpose is to determine the origin and inner structure of the American Negro folksong; the conclusion is that both African and American sources were drawn upon. Includes a chapter concerning structural analysis of the spiritual.

160. Cumming, Janet. *An Annotated Bibliography Relating to the Study of the Dance.* Wisconsin, M.S. (phy. ed.), 1939. Pp. 67.

161. Czarnowski, Lucille. *Some Genetic Phases of the Dance.* Wisconsin, M.S. (phy. ed.), 1931.

162. Daniel, Vattel Elbert. *Ritual in Chicago's South Side Churches for Negroes.* Chicago, Ph.D. (sociol.), 1940. Pp. 155. *Pub.*: (in part) under the title "Ritual and Stratification in Chicago Negro Churches," *Amer. Sociol. Rev.* 7 (1942), pp. 352-361.
> Use of "sermons, prayers, songs and behavior in studying the ceremonials and beliefs of types of communicants representing class and economic differences in urban Negro life."

163. Daniell, Martha Louise. *Sixteen Play-Party Songs from Randolph County, West Virginia.* Ohio State U., M.A. (music), 1943.

164. Darack, Arthur. *Aesthetics of Music: Early Greek Views.* Indiana U., Ph.D. (music theory), 1951. Pp. 181, *D.A.* XIV, 2363.
> The purpose of the author is to "attempt a systematic expression of significant statements of a philosophy of music from pre-Socratic to the peripatetic philosophers." The period dealt with is approximately 600 to 300 B.C.

165. Daugherty, George Henry, Jr. *Reflections of Environment in North American Indian Literature.* Chicago, Ph.D. (engl.), 1925.
> Considers songs and ritual orations of Indians in general, primarily Chippewa, Sioux, Pima and some Iroquois.

166. Daum, Hubert. *Soziologie der Musik, Ansätze und Probleme.* Graz (phil.), 1958. Pp. 141, 3.

167. David, Reginald Charles. *Canadian Folksongs for American Schools*. Eastman, M.M. (music ed.), 1950. Pp. iv, 176, music and texts of 59 songs.
   > Following a short discussion of Canada's musical heritage, the author analyzes the text and music of Canadian Eskimo and Indian folksongs, French-Canadian folksongs, and the sea songs and ballads of Canada's East Coast.

168. Davidson, Frank Costellow. *The Rise, Development, Decline and Influence of the American Minstrel Show*. New York U., Ph.D. (speech), 1952. Pp. 276. *D.A.* XIII, 268.
   > "It was concluded that the minstrel show is the only indigenous American contribution to the drama, and that the melodies the Negro ministrel inspired are America's only approach to national music."

169. Davidson, Robert Nathaniel. *A Study of the Ghost Dance of 1889*. Stanford U., M.A., 1952. Pp. 49.

170. Davis, Ouida Pauline. *A Study of the Terminology of American Country Dances*. Texas, M.A. (phy. ed.), 1940. Pp. 134.

171. Dees, Levi O. *Social Development of the Secular Musician*. Northwestern U., M.M., 1936.

172. Dempe, Rolf. *Die syrischen Hymnen von Ephrem*. Jena (phil.), 1958. Pp. iv, 501, music.

173. Denis, P. *De stand van het onderzoek der muziek in Belgisch Congo*. Ghent, Licentiate, 1955.

174. Der Hovhannissian, Harpik. *Armenian Music: A Cosmopolitan Art*. Florida State U., Ph.D. (music), 1956. 2 vols. Pp. 292. *D.A.* XVI, 2475.
   > Discusses church, folk and art music with some attention to folk dances and musical instruments.

175. DeShone, Thomas Jake. *Dance Bands and Public School Music*. Northwestern U., M.M., 1954.

176. Devine, George John. *American Songsters, 1806-1815*. Brown U., M.A. (engl.), 1940.
   > A continuation of the Alice Louise Thorpe and Arthur Ansel Lewis theses. See under Thorpe for annotation.

177. Divers, Jessyca Pauline. *The African Methodist Episcopal Church and Its Hymnal.* Northwestern U., M.M., 1944.

178. Döhrn, Gisela. *Die Volksliedbearbeitungen von Johannes Brahms.* Vienna (phil.), 1936.

179. Doğanç, Ayhan H. *Folk Taste and Judgment as Revealed in Turkish Folksongs.* Indiana U., M.A. (folkl.), 1963. Pp. iv, 119, bibliog.

Author worked with 800 song texts and 462 texts with music, collected from informants in Turkey and from broadsides and songbooks. The approach is literary and the problems of origin, dissemination and variations are not handled.

180. Donahue, Margaret. *A Course of Music Study for Indian Children.* South Dakota, M.A. (music), 1944.

181. Donaldson, Martha. *Primitive Motivations of the Dance.* Geo. Peabody, M.A. (phy. ed.), 1936. Pp. 129.

182. Dorndorf, Anton Hubert. *Historical Analysis of the German-American Singing Societies in California, with an Evaluation.* Pacific, M.A. (music), 1955. Pp. 300.

183. Dorrum, Eleanor Valborg. *A Study of Selected Norwegian Folk Songs with Special Reference to Their Adaptation for High School Mixed Chorus.* Iowa, M.A. (music), 1942. Pp. 62.

184. Downey, John Witham. *La Musique populaire dans l'oeuvre de Béla Bartók.* Paris, thèse lettres, 1956. 2 vols. Pp. vi, 540, 420 music exs. Ronéotypés. *D.A.* XXIII, 4650.

In three parts, the first is an analytical survey of folk music sources with which Bartók himself came in contact: Hungarian, Romanian, Slovak, Arabian, Ukrainian, Bulgarian, Serbo-Croatian and Turkish. Folk melody structures, isometric and isorhythmic traits, intervallic and modal peculiarities, range and melodic contour, and especially rhythmic patterns are analyzed. These factors are also treated in part two where Bartók's use of these elements in his own works is considered. Part three is not available on microfilm.

185. Doyle, John Godfrey. *The Piano Music of Louis Moreau Gottschalk (1829-1869).* New York U., Ph.D. (music ed.), 1960. Pp. 184. *D.A.* XXI, 3113.

An attempt to identify melodic and rhythmic characteristics of Louisiana Creole and Latin American folk music in Gottschalk's piano compositions. Includes a Thematic Index (105 compositions) and a study of the principal characteristics of his musical style.

186. Dräger, Hans Heinz. *Prinzip einer Systematik der Musikinstrumente.* Kiel (HabSchr.), 1946. *Pub.: Musikwiss. Arbeiten* 3 (Kassel, Bärenreiter-Verlag, 1948). Pp. 49.

187. Drubeck, Ida M. *Ritual Music of the Jewish Synagogue.* Wisconsin, M.A. (music), 1937.

188. Drüner, Otto. *Die deutsche Volksballade in Lothringen. Beiträge zur Erforschung ihrer Weisen.* (Nebst) Anhang: Notenbeispiele mit Quellennachweis. Frankfurt a.M. (phil.), 1937 (1939). *Pub.: Schriften d. Wiss. Inst. d. Elsass-Lothringer im Reich an d. Univ. Frankfurt,* N.F. 21 (Frankfurt a. M., Diesterweg, 1939). Pp. xv, 137, 36.

189. Drummond, Isabel N. *A Study of the Literary and Artistic Elements of the Life of the Sioux.* Indiana U., M.A. (engl.), 1930. Pp. viii, 137, bibliog.
    Pages 92-112 deal with the ceremonial (ritual, religious, individual), social, and folk music of the Sioux, based entirely on published material by Densmore.

190. Duerksen, Rosella Reimer. *Anabaptist Hymnody of the 16th Century; A Study of Its Marked Individuality, Coupled with a Dependence Upon Contemporary Secular and Sacred Musical Style and Form.* Union Theol. Sem., D.S.M., 1956.

191. Durham, Lovell M. *The Role and History of Music in the Mormon Church.* Iowa, M.A. (music), 1942.

192. Duvall, Miriam Reed. *Contemporary Attitudes and Habits in Social Dancing.* Geo. Peabody, M.A. (phy. ed.), 1937. Pp. 87.

193. Echezona, William Wilberforce Chukudinka. *Ibo Musical Instruments in Ibo Culture.* Michigan State, Ph.D. (music), 1963. Pp. 214, 39 figures, 36 photo. pls. *D.A.* XXV, 1246. *Pub.:* (in part) *Music Educators J.* 50 (April-May, 1964), pp. 23-27, 130, 131.
    Using the Sachs-Hornbostel classification, instruments used for social and religious events and for communication, and instruments having therapeutic qualities are discussed.

26

194. Eckardt, Hans. *Das "Kokonchomonshū" des Tachibana Narisue als musikgeschichtliche Quelle.* Berlin, F.U. (HabSchr.), 1954. *Pub.*: *Göttinger asiatische Forschungen* 6 (Leipzig, Harrassowitz, 1956). Pp. 432.

195. Economo, Konstantin. *Studien über das neugriechische Volkslied.* Munich (phil.), 1928.

196. Edelman, Daniel. *The Urban Music of the Ottoman Turks.* Boston U., M.A., 1954. Pp. 94, music, texts.

    Devoted to the technical aspects of the music divided into seven types; scales, notation system, modes, rhythmic patterns, poetry, instruments, and other factors are considered.

197. Edelman, Daniel. *The Tonal System of Turkish Classical Music and a Descriptive Analysis of the Principal Makams (Modes).* Indiana U., Ph.D. (music). In process.

198. Eidbo, Olav Elling. *Songs of the Norwegian Folk in Culture and Education in the United States.* North Dakota, Ph.D. (educ.), 1956. Pp. 354, figs., music, tables.

    Historical, normative-survey (questionnaire), descriptive research and personal interview methods were used in the study of individuals, organizations and publications which have served to present, preserve and propagate folk and ethnic songs peculiar to Norwegian-Americans. 100 folk, ballad and art songs, with melodies and appropriate Norwegian texts (some English translations), are included in an appendix.

199. Elephant, Adriana. *Die musikalische Gattungsbestimmung des rumänischen Volksliedes.* Munich (phil.), 1937.

200. El Kholy, S. A. *The Function of Music in Islamic Culture (in the Period up to A.D. 1100).* Edinburgh, Ph.D., 1953-1954.

201. Ellis, Catharine J. *A Study of Central Australian Music.* Glasgow, Ph.D. (music), 1961. Pp. 368, bibliog., "Catalogue of Rhythms," charts, graphs, music, tables. *Pub.*: Adelaide, Libraries Board of South Australia, 1964. Pp. 404.

    The main portion is a detailed analysis, including full transcriptions and pitch measurements, of portions of 18 Central Australian men's sacred ceremonies, from recordings made by T. G. H. Strehlow. Other sections deal with relevant extra-musical information, discussions of other writings on Australian Aboriginal music, and brief references to present-day part-Aboriginal creative output.

202. Ellison, Alfred. *The Composer under Twentieth Century Political Ideologies.* Columbia U., Ph.D., 1950.

Educational implications in National Socialist Germany, the Soviet Union and the United States.

203. Emery, Eric. *Les Gammes et les problèmes d'esthétique musicale qui s'y rapportent.* Zurich (L'École Polytechnique), 1961. *Pub.:* Paris, Presses Universitaires, 1961. Pp. 164, bibliog., illus.

204. Empey, Louella Jeanette. *Spanish Folk Music as Source Material for Religious Education.* Chicago, M.A. (music), 1931. Pp. 119, music.

205. Eneboe, Rose Adelaide. *The Musical Aptitude of Seven Hundred and Forty High School Students of Different Nationalities.* Northwestern U., M.S. (educ.), 1933. Pp. 53.

Includes Austrian, British, Czech, Danish, Dutch, French, German, Greek, Hungarian, Irish, Italian, Lithuanian, Norwegian, Russian, Slavic and Swedish groups.

206. Engelke, Hans. *A Study of Ornaments in American Tune-Books, 1760-1800.* So. California, Ph.D. (music), 1960. Pp. 217, *D.A.* XX, 4130.

Includes references to singing practices in the Colonies, and influences on the interpretation of ornaments in the tune-books.

207. England, Nicholas M. *Music in the Societies of Certain Groups of Bushmen in South Africa.* Harvard, Ph.D. In process.

208. Erdely, Stephen. *An Essay on Methods and Principles of Hungarian Ethnomusicology.* Western Reserve U., Ph.D. (musicol.), 1962. Pp. 189, bibliog., music, tables.

Kodály's four studies, *Strophic Structure of Hungarian Folksong, Pentatonism in Hungarian Folksong, Characteristic Melodic Structure in Cheremis Folksong,* and *Folk Music of Hungary* are evaluated, critically compared, and extended by new research on the part of the writer.

209. Erneston, Nicholas. *A Study to Determine the Effect of Musical Experience and Mental Ability on the Formulation of Musical Taste.* Florida State U., Ph.D. (music), 1961. Pp. 176. *D.A.* XXII, 2817.

A study involving 780 college freshmen at Appalachian State Teachers College in Boone, North Carolina, during the academic year 1960-1961. The findings suggested that there was a strong relationship between musical experience and acquired musical taste and that high mental ability contributes positively to taste formulation.

210. Espina, A. Beaunoni. *Music in the Philippines and the Development of Sacred Music There.* Union Theol. Sem., D.S.M., 1961. Pp. xxvi, 314, bibliog., illus., maps, music, tables.

The early part of the work, dealing with the music of various cultural groups on the islands, will be of especial interest to ethnomusicologists.

211. Estreicher, Zygmunt. *La Musique des Esquimaux-Caribous.* Freiburg i. Br., Ph.D., 1948.

212. Etzkorn, Peter Klaus. *Musical and Social Patterns of Songwriters: An Exploratory Sociological Study.* Princeton U., Ph.D. (sociol.), 1959. Pp. 349. *D.A.* XXI, 1281.

Results of Dennison Nash's study of twenty-three American composers are contrasted with the data obtained by interview and questionnaire returns from twenty-five successful songwriters of 1958. Includes an analysis of the sheet music of forty songs of which a million or more recordings had been sold.

213. Evans, Ruth Harriet. *Music of India.* Wisconsin, M. Phil., 1937. Pp. 113, bibliog., music, tables.

Includes chapters concerning history, scales, *ragas, talas,* instruments, notation, composition, and Indian and Western music.

214. Farhat, Hormoz. *The "Dastgah" Concept in Persian Classical Music.* California (Los Angeles), Ph.D. In process.

215. Farrow, Charlotte. *The Communist Attitude Toward Music: Its Roots in History, Its Philosophical Basis and Its Growth Within Soviet Culture from 1917 to the Present.* Northwestern U., M.M., 1954. Pp. iv, 156, bibliog.

Approached from the point of view that the communist attitude toward music is a theory of art which is a recurring pattern with roots leading back from modern communism to the Reformation, to the Medieval Church and finally to Plato.

216. Faurot, Albert Louis. *Music in the Chinese Church.* Oberlin, M.A. (theol.), 1940. Pp. 120.

217. Felber, Erwin. *Die indische Musik der vedischen und klassischen Zeit. Nach den Platten des Phonogramm-Archivs der*

Akademie. Mit Texten und Übersetzung von Bernhard Geiger.
Vienna (phil.), 1911. *Pub.: Sitzungsbericht der Akad. der Wissenschaften, Phil.-hist. Klasse,* 170, *Abhandlung* 7 (Vienna, Akademie der Wissenschaften, 1912).

218. Fenton, William Nelson. *The Seneca Eagle Dance; A Study of Personality Expression in Ritual.* Yale, Ph.D. (anthro.), 1937. Pp. 264. *Pub.:* under the title *The Iroquois Eagle Dance, an Offshoot of the Calumet Dance.* U.S. Bur. Amer. Ethnol., Bull. 156 (Wash., D.C., 1953). Pp. 324, bibliog., figs., illus., pls.
     Incorporates ethnographic materials gathered during field work in western New York between 1933 and 1936.

219. Ferand, Ernest T. *Die Improvisationspraxis in der Musik. I. Teil: Von den Anfängen bis um 1600.* Vienna (phil.), 1936. *Pub.:* under the title *Die Improvisation in der Musik. Eine entwicklungs-geschichtliche und psychologische Untersuchung.* Zürich, Rhein-Verl., 1939. Pp. xiv, 464.

220. Fillies, Walter. *Die Arbeitersängerbewegung. Ein Beitrag zur Klassengeschichte der Arbeiterschaft.* Rostock (phil.), 1922. Pp. 191.

221. Finesinger, Sol Baruch. *Musical Instruments in the Old Testament.* Johns Hopkins U., Ph.D., 1925. *Pub.: Hebrew Union College Annual* 3 (1926), pp. 21-76, bibliog., figs., tables.
     A variety of sources was used in describing Ancient Hebrew musical instruments and comparing them with Egyptian, Assyrian and, occasionally, Greek instruments. The author reviews past attempts at identifying the instruments and states his own opinions and preferences.

222. Fischer, Erich. *Beiträge zur Erforschung der chinesischen Musik nach phonographischen Aufnahmen.* Berlin (phil.), 1910. Pp. 30, 24.

223. Fischer, Hans. *Schallgeräte in Ozeanien; Bau und Spieltechnik, Verbreitung und Funktion.* Hamburg (phil.), 1956. Pp. v, 244. *Pub.: Collection d'études musicologiques,* 36 (Strasbourg, P. H. Heitz, 1958). Pp. 177, bibliog., illus., tables.
     Attempts to give a complete distribution of instruments, giving data on the instruments and on their role in musical and ceremonial life, but not on the style of the music.

224. Fischer, Ruby Keefauver (Mrs.). *Literary and Artistic Expression of the Hopi Indians.* Indiana U., M.A. (engl.), 1930. Pp. v, 141.

> Chapter V, part 2 (pp. 108-115): Song and Poetry, based entirely on an early work by Voth.

225. Fisher, Miles Mark. *The Evolution of Slave Songs of the United States.* Chicago, Ph.D. (Divinity School), 1948. Pp. 350. *Pub.:* (rev. and enl.) under the title *Negro Slave Songs in the United States* (Ithaca, Cornell U. Press, for the Amer. Hist. Assoc., 1953). Pp. xv, 223, bibliog., no music.

> A "discussion of Negro folksongs as folk music and as proof of various theories about the Negro." Includes analysis of a number of well-known antebellum spirituals.

226. Fleischhauer, Günter. *Die Musikergenossenschaften im hellenistischrömischen Altertum. Beiträge zum Musikleben der Römer.* Halle (phil.), 1960. Pp. 229.

227. Foley, Rolla. *The Religious Ceremonies, Shrines, and Folk Music of the Holy Land Christians.* So. California, M.M., 1951. Pp. 217, music.

> Chapter XII includes transcriptions, without analysis, of Arabian religious music.

228. Foley, Rolla. *Work Songs of the Arab.* Columbia T.C., Ph.D., 1956. Pp. 344.

> Africa and Asia.

229. Forbes, Kenneth V. A. *A Chapter from the Story of Early Vermont Music.* Iowa, M.A. (music), 1927. Pp. x, 186.

> An attempt at a collection of the music in common use in rural Franklin County, Vt., during the middle part of the nineteenth century. Based to a small extent on original transcriptions, partly on printed material of Vermont origin, mostly on non-Vermont material.

230. Fosbury, Evelyn. *Jewish Folk Music.* Northwestern U., M.M., 1951. Pp. vi, 89, bibliog., music.

> Discussion of Jewish folk music of the Oriental and Sephardic, and Western and Eastern Ashkenazic Jews, as well as of modern Palestine. Also chapters on Jewish folk music before the Dispersion, and the place of Jewish folksong in the creation of a Jewish national music.

31

231. Foster, William P. *The Influence of the Negro on Music in America.* Wayne State U., M.A. (music), 1950. Pp. 128, music.
Detailed analysis of African elements in American cultivated music, and jazz. The discussion of African music and methods of analysis are not based on the best sources, and important literature is neglected.

232. Fouché, Ruth Allen. *Transitional Qualities in Puerto Rican Folk Music.* Chicago Mus. Coll., M.A., 1954.
Presents contemporary survivals of African chant in description and disc recording together with the largely prevailing Spanish-Puerto Rican folksongs.

233. Freeburg, Roy Everett Walter. *The Use of Musical Resources of the Pacific-Southwest Region for Elementary Education.* Stanford U., Ed.D., 1946. Pp. 334, bibliog.
The material is selective rather than comprehensive, and includes information for Pacific-Southwest Indians on songs, legends, stories, and how people reveal their habits, customs and ideals through their songs of worship, work, play and travel.

234. Friedrich, Wilhelm. *Die älteste türkische Beschreibung von Musikinstrumenten aus dem Anfang des 15. Jahrhunderts von Ahmedoglu Šükrülläh.* Breslau (phil.), 1944. Pp. iv, 125.

235. Frings, Wilhelm. *Vom Musikalisch-Schönen im deutschen Volkslied.* Bonn (phil.), 1915. *Pub.:* Bonn, Rhenania-Verl., 1915. Pp. 36.

236. Fritsch, M. *Das Volkslied im Egerland.* Prague (phil.), 1940. Pp. 172.

237. Fritz, John Carolus. *A Comparison of Musical Capacity and Musical Achievement of Spanish-American and American Pupils in Morenci Junior High School.* Arizona, M.A., 1940. Pp. 42.

238. Frye, Grace Tener. *The Revival of the Folk Dance as Social Recreation in Northern California.* Pacific, M.A. (phy. ed.), 1947. Pp. 113.

239. Fukudo, Hanako. *Lullabies of the Western Hemisphere.* So. California, Ed.D., 1960. Pp. 495. *D.A.* XXI, 496.
154 samples, representing twenty-eight groups of people, were studied in an attempt to show similarities in ranges and usage of tones, melodic repetition, rhythms, and sentiment expressed in the text of the song.

240. Furnas, Philip W. *Serbo-Croatian Folk Songs*. Harvard, Ph.D., 1939.

241. Gamble, John Irvin. *Kiowa Dance Gatherings and Costumed Dancers*. Washington U., M.A., 1952. Pp. 78.

242. Gamble, Margaret. *The Heritage and Folk Music of Cades Cove, Tennessee*. So. California, M.M., 1947. Pp. 242.

243. Gamo, S. *A Study of the Melody of Nagauta*. Tokyo U. Arts, 1960.

244. Gangware, Edgar Brand, Jr. *The History and Use of Percussion Instruments in Orchestration*. Northwestern U., Ph.D. (music), 1962. Pp. 292. D.A. XXIII, 4707.
    Traces the historical development of percussion instruments from antiquity through the study of numerous illustrations from early civilizations, ancient instruments, some of the earliest writings concerning music, and many articles which were in part significant.

245. Gardner, Anna Elizabeth. *A Study of Certain Phases of Musical Ability in Young Children of Different Nationalities*. New York S. C. for Teachers, M.A., 1930. Pp. 38.
    Includes British, German, Irish, Italian, Scandinavian, and Slavic groups.

246. Garfias, Robert. *Certain Features of the Gagaku Music of Japan*. California (Los Angeles), Ph.D. In process.

247. Garner, Netta P. *A Survey of the Music and Instruments of Equatorial Africa*. So. California, M.M., 1951. Pp. 142, map, music.
    A study of the part music plays in the lives of the people, and the value of such study to music students. Based on secondary sources with no new transcriptions.

248. Garrell, Harriet. *Origin, History, Classification and Significance of the Spanish Dance*. Geo. Peabody, M.A. (phy. ed.), 1937.

249. Gehlhoff, Gerhard. *Beiträge zur Entwicklung von Volksliedmelodien. (Eine vergleichende Liedstudie.)* Berlin (phil.), 1923. Summary in *Jahrb. d. Diss. d. Phil. Fak. Berlin*, 1922/23, I, pp. 274-277.

250. Gellatly, Marjorie Gail. *Fourteen Northwest Coast Indian Songs Transcribed into Musical Notation*. Washington, M.A. (music ed.), 1940. Pp. iii, 79, bibliog., music.

> There is a brief description of each song ethnographically, but no musicological analysis. The author states that the songs are notated in the system suggested by George Herzog.

251. George, Zelma Watson. *A Guide to Negro Music: An Annotated Bibliography of Negro Folk Music, and Art Music by Negro Composers or Based on Negro Thematic Material*. New York U., Ed.D. (music), 1953. Pp. 302. *D.A. XIV, 841.*

> Part I: 12,163 titles located in the Howard University Library; Part II: A comprehensive critical analysis of the literature about the various aspects of Negro music research, from the historico-ethnosocio-musicological approach.

252. Georgiades, Thrasybulos. *Bemerkungen zur antiken Quantitätsmetrik*. Munich (HabSchr.), 1947. *Pub.*: under the title *Der griechische Rhythmus: Musik, Reigen, Vers und Sprache*. Hamburg, M. von Schröder, 1949.

253. Geutebrück, Robert. *Über Form und Rhythmus des älteren deutschen Volksgesanges*. Vienna (phil.), 1925. *Pub.*: (in part) *AfMw* 7 (1925), pp. 337-411.

254. Gillis, Frank James. *Minnesota Music in the Nineteenth Century: A Guide to Sources and Resources*. Minnesota, M.A. (lib. sci.), 1958. Pp. vii, 91, illus.

> Discusses sources relating to Indian music and to the music of the early European settlers.

255. Gillum, Ruth Helen. *The Negro Folk Song and Its Influence in America*. Kansas, M.A. (music), 1940. Pp. 144.

256. Gizzarelli, Ermanno Francis. *An Historical Survey of Italian Folk Song and a Critical Estimate of Modern Research*. Cornell U., Ph.D. (musicol.), 1938. Pp. xxxi, 185, bibliog., music.

> Following a brief historical survey of European folksong, the author examines and evaluates general and regional collections of Italian folksong from the fourteenth to the nineteenth centuries. An attempt is made to determine (1) whether melodies actually have folk quality or are the products of sophisticated art; (2) whether the particular collections of folksong are selective or exhaustive; and (3) whether the presentation is in keeping with the spirit of folk art or has been obscured by additions of a compiler. Considerable attention is given to laude, frottole and villanelle.

257. Glazer, Irving William. *Negro Music in Early America, from 1619 to the Civil War.* New York U., M.A. (music), 1945. Pp. 99.

258. Göllner, Konrad Rudolf August. *Die Volksmusik Norwegens als Grundlage des Schaffens Edvard Griegs.* Vienna (phil.), 1940. Pp. viii, 295.

259. Göpel, Alfred. *Der Wandel des Kinderliedes im 18. Jahrhundert.* Kiel (phil.), 1935. Pp. 68, 4. *Pub.*: Quakenbruck, R. Kleinert, 1935. Pp. 72, music.

260. Gold, Charles E. *A Study of the Gospel Song.* So. California, M.M., 1953. Pp. 126, music.
    The purpose is: 1) to differentiate between the terms "hymn" and "gospel song"; 2) to present a historical study; 3) to study the pertinent scriptural terms "psalms, hymns, and spiritual songs"; 4) to analyze both text and music. The thesis concentrates on the white revival tradition.

261. Goldstein, Kenneth S. *A Guide for Field Workers in Folklore.* Pennsylvania, Ph.D. (folkl.), 1963. Pp. 277, bibliog. *D.A.* XXIV, 1974. *Pub.*: Hatboro, Penna., Folklore Associates, 1964. Pp. xviii, 199.
    A systematic presentation of the methods and techniques used in collecting folklore data and materials. Much of what is given applicable to the collecting of music materials.

262. Goranowski, Helen. *An Analysis of 65 Polish Folk-Songs; with Conclusions Based on This Analysis Concerning the Relation Between Language Rhythms and Music Rhythms; and Concerning the Evolution and Transplantation of These Songs to America.* Wayne State U., M.A. (music), 1951. Pp. 220, maps, music, tables.
    Background information on informants, introduction on folk music and Polish immigration to the United States; analysis of the music; comparison of Polish songs brought from Poland with others learned in the United States.

263. Gordon, Diane Kestin. *Folklore in Modern English Opera.* California (Los Angeles), Ph.D. (music), 1959. 2 vols., bibliog., music.
    Traces the use of folklore and folk music as used in modern English opera.

264. Gould, Cassius Wallace. *An Analysis of the Folk-Music in the Oaxaca and Chiapas Areas of Mexico.* Northwestern U., Ph.D. (music), 1954. Pp. xii, 314, bibliog., 25 figs., 33 music exs. *D.A.* XIV, 2085.

> Based on field research, the dissertation deals with the transcription and analysis of music of the areas noted. Special attention is given to its relationships with pre-Cortesian music.

265. Gower, (Lemuel) Herschel. *Traditional Scottish Ballads in the United States.* Vanderbilt U., Ph.D. (engl. lit.), 1957. Pp. 228. *D.A.* XVII, 1750.

> Using Child's *English and Scottish Popular Ballads,* this study "endeavors to classify English and Scottish ballads as to national origin and to make a clear delineation in American balladry that has not heretofore been attempted." Conclusion is that "at least forty per cent of the Child ballads collected in the U.S. are of Scottish origin."

266. Graf, Walter. *Über den deutschen Einfluss auf den estnischen Volksgesang.* Vienna (phil.), 1932.

267. Grannaway, Mary Ann. *Singing Games of Cumberland Mountain, Tennessee.* Geo. Peabody, M.A. (educ.), 1935.

268. Grant, Philip S. *Songs of the Forty-Niners.* California, M.A., 1925.

269. Grauer, Victor. *Hebrew Chant in the Daily Liturgy of the Synagogue.* Wesleyan U., M.A., 1961.

270. Green, Beryl A. *Folk Music in Jamaica, British West Indies.* Wayne State U., M.A., 1951.

271. Greenberg, Marvin. *Music Education in Israel in Its Cultural and Educational Contexts: A Survey with Recommendations for Future Growth.* Columbia U., Ed.D. (music), 1962. Pp. 494. *D.A.* XXIII, 4376.

> The findings presented are based on research in Israel.

272. Greene, Barbara Joyce. *African Musical Survivals in the Songs of the Negro in Haiti, Jamaica and the United States.* Chicago, A.M. (anthro.), 1948. Pp. 114, music, tables.

> Research for this study was done at Columbia University under George Herzog, by agreement with the Department of Anthropology at the University of Chicago. The study "attempts to

show how the music of one people has changed in three contact situations," specifically, the music of the West Africans in Haiti, Jamaica and the United States.

273. Greenway, John. *American Folksongs of Social and Economic Protest*. Pennsylvania, Ph.D. (engl. lit.), 1951. *Pub.*: Philadelphia, Univ. of Pa. Press, 1953. Pp. x, 348, bibliog., indexes, music.

> Songs of the Negro, textile worker, miner, migrant worker, farmer, and laborer are treated. The final chapter, "The Song Makers," includes discussions of Woody Guthrie, Joe Glazer and other makers of folksongs.

274. Gregg, Katherine. *Musical Instruments of the Troubadours*. Wisconsin, M.A. (music), 1935.

275. Grieser, Heinz. *Nomos. Ein Beitrag zur griechischen Musikgeschichte*. Heidelberg (phil.), 1937. *Pub.*: *Quellen u. Studien z. Gesch. u. Kultur d. Altertums u. d. Mittelalters*, D, 5 (Heidelberg, Bilabel, 1937). Pp. 73.

276. Gröger, Helene. *Die Musikinstrumente im Kult der Afrikaner*. Vienna (phil.), 1946. Pp. xi, 289.

277. Grotts, Pearl Irene. *Sociological Aspects of the Crow Indian Dances*. Iowa, M.A. (phy. ed.), 1942. Pp. 23.

278. Guelig, Evangeline. *The Effects of Music on the Socially Maladjusted*. Northwestern U., M.M., 1943.

279. Günther, Robert. *Musik in Ruanda. Ein Beitrag zur Musikethnologie Zentral-afrikas*. Cologne (phil.), 1960. *Pub.*: Tervuren, Musée Royal de l'Afrique Centrale, 1964. Bibliog., music, photos.

> The emphasis is on music more than ethnology, with analysis and transcriptions and photographs of instruments being played. There is a French summary included.

280. Guild, Elliott William. *The Sociological Role of Music in Primitive Cultures*. Stanford U., M.A. (econ.), 1931. Pp. 127.

> "In primitive life . . . the lives of these people were steeped in music. . . . There was no form of primitive culture in which music did not play a part. . . . In its rise to a powerful agency of social control and to its position as a vital role in primitive man's drama it became coterminous with group life."

281. Gunst, Marie Louise. *Ceremonials of the Papago and Pima Indians, with Special Emphasis on the Relationship of the Dance to Their Religion.* Arizona, M.A., 1930. Pp. 73.

282. Gutfleisch, Albert. *Volkslied in der Jugendbewegung, betrachtet am Zupfgeigenhansl.* Frankfurt a.M. (phil.), 1934. Pp. 86.

283. Haager, Max. *Die instrumentale Volksmusik im Salzkammergut.* Vienna (phil.), 1931.

284. Haddox, Clara Gibson. *A Study of the Customs, Folkways and Folk Dances of Mexico.* Geo. Peabody, M.A., 1952. Pp. 97.
    Includes Aztec and Maya.

285. Hagen, Karl. *Über die Musik einiger Naturvölker (Australier, Melanesier, Polynesier).* Jena (phil.), 1892. Pp. 35.

286. Hakuta, N. *Musical Form in India.* Tokyo U. Arts, 1959.

287. Hale, Harry Morgan. *A Study of the Musical Talents of Hawaiian, Filipino, and Portuguese Children.* Hawaii, M.A., 1936. Pp. 68.
    As a follow-up to F. B. Johnson's thesis, this study was also based on the Seashore tests. The author's conclusions show, first, that there is no significant correlation between general intelligence and musical capacity; secondly, that although one group rated slightly higher (Filipino), and one group slightly lower (Portuguese), the three tested groups of youngsters proved to be very similar in musical capacity.

288. Hallowell, Alfred Irving. *Bear Ceremonialism in the Northern Hemisphere.* Pennsylvania, Ph.D. (anthro.), 1924. *Pub.: Amer. Anthro.* 28 (1926), pp. 1-175, bibliog.
    Occasional references to song and dance (and to sources dealing with these subjects) in a number of culture areas.

289. Hammond, Stella Lou. *Contribution of the American Indian and Negro to the Folk-Music of America.* Wayne State U., M.A. (music), 1936. Pp. 97, music.
    Very general description of American Indian and Negro music, their influence on American cultivated music, and their role in American folk music at large.

38

290. Hampton, Janet Edwards. *Customs and Origins of Certain Folk Dances.* So. California, M.A. (phy. ed.), 1933. Pp. 96, bibliog.

> Based on library research, interviews with directors of folk dance groups, and correspondence with foreign authorities.

291. Hanschke, Hans Gerhard. *Studien über die melodisch-harmonischen Beziehungen im neuen Gemeinschaftsliede.* Erlangen (phil.), 1940. Pp. 47.

292. Hansen, Chadwick Clarke. *The Ages of Jazz: A Study of Jazz in Its Cultural Context.* Minnesota, Ph.D. (american studies), 1956. Pp. 213, bibliog. *D.A.* XX, 2324.

> Dealing, generally, with the role of the Negro in the development of jazz, the study covers African backgrounds, early beginnings in the New World, New Orleans, Chicago, and such style periods as swing and bop.

293. Hanson, William F. *The Lure of Tam-man Nacup, Springtime Festival of the Utes.* Brigham Young U., M.S. (music), 1937. Pp. 179, illus., music, plates.

> Tam-man Nacup (Spring is coming) is the annual ceremonial Bear Dance of the Unitah, in which the dance represents not only the joy of the Bear after a long winter's sleep, but the actual pageant of his "coming," of the sun's return to the south, and a general rebirth of nature at springtime. Words and music of the festival are included in the appendix.

294. Harbert, Wilhelmina Keniston. *Some Principles, Practices and Techniques in Musical Therapy.* Pacific, M.A. (psych.), 1947. Pp. 132.

295. Harich-Schneider, Eta. *The Relations of Foreign and Native Elements in the Development of Japanese Music; A Case Study.* New School for Social Res., M.A. (pol. and soc. sci.), 1954. Pp. 112, bibliog., music.

> A study of foreign influence and native reactions to it during the two great periods when foreign cultures were introduced: Chinese culture from the sixth to eighth centuries, A.D., and Western culture during the nineteenth century.

296. Harper, Jean. *A Comparative Study of American Country Dance and Foreign Folk Dance in American Colleges and Universities of the United States.* Smith C., M.S., 1948.

297. Harpham, Ornal Zane. *A Study to Determine the Value of Music as a Therapeutic Agent in the Rehabilitation of a Schizophrenic.* Pacific, M.A. (music), 1951. Pp. 168.

298. Hartman, Elizabeth Rose. *A Project for Making the Musical Instruments Used in Solomon's Temple, with Suggested Programs of Lectures and Music.* Union Theol. Sem., M.A. (music), 1943.

299. Hartmann, Artur. *Untersuchungen über metrisches Verhalten in musikalischen Interpretationsvarianten. Ein Beitrag zur Musikpsychologie.* Hamburg (phil.), 1932. *Pub.: Archiv f. d. gesamte Psychologie* 84, pp. 103-192.

300. Hartmann, Henrike. *Die Musik der sumerischen Kultur.* Frankfurt a.M. (phil.), 1958. Pp. 388, bibliog., illus., map.

301. Hattori, K. *Musical Form of the "Kangen" in Japanese Court Music.* Tokyo U. Arts, 1956.

302. Haugen, Myrtle. *An Adaptation of Scandinavian Folk and National Songs for Use in American Schools.* Northwestern U., M.S. (educ.), 1933.

303. Haupt, Else. *Stil und sprachkundliche Untersuchungen zum deutschen Schlager; unter besonderer Berücksichtigung des Vergleichs mit dem deutschen Volkslied.* Munich (phil.), 1957. Pp. ii, 130.

304. Hause, Helen Engel. *Terms for Musical Instruments in the Sudanic Languages; A Lexicographical Inquiry.* Pennsylvania, Ph.D., 1948. Pp. 88. *Pub.: J. of the Amer. Oriental Soc.,* Supp. no. 7 (1948). Pp. 71, bibliog.

305. Hayden, Alice. *An Appreciation of the Folk Dance.* Geo. Peabody, M.A. (phy. ed.), 1931. Pp. 107.

306. Haywood, Charles. *Bibliography of North American Folklore and Folksong.* Columbia U., Ph.D., 1951. Pp. 1292 (double column), intro., index, maps. *Pub.:* N. Y., Greenberg 1951. *Repub.:* N. Y., Dover, 1961. Vol. I: Pp. xxx, 748; Vol. II: Pp. ix, 1301; corrected and enlarged by a supplementary index of composers, arrangers and performers.
 A comprehensive roundup of over 40,000 entries of printed sources covering every aspect of folklore and folksong. Volume I examines song, dance, and recordings of various ethnic groups, occupations, etc. Volume II deals with the Indians north of Mexico. Cut-off date is 1948.

307. Heidenreich, Margaret A. *A Study of American Folk Music for Sixth, Seventh, and Eighth Grade Boys and Girls.* So. California, M.M., 1952. Pp. 253.
      Illustrates music the author feels is directed to the specific interests of children of this age group.

308. Heidsieck, Ralph. *The Music of the Southern California Indians: Its Significance, Selected Transcriptions, and Development in the Elementary School Curriculum.* California (Los Angeles), Ph.D. In process.

309. Heilfurth, Gerhard. *Das erzgebirgische Bergmannslied. Ein Aufriss seiner literarischen Geschichte.* Leipzig (phil.), 1936. *Pub.*: Schwarzenberg, Glückauf Verl., 1936. Pp. 143, illus., music, tables.

310. Heinitz, Wilhelm. *Strukturprobleme in primitiver Musik.* Hamburg (HabSchr.), 1931. *Pub.*: Hamburg, Friederichsen, de Gruyter, 1931. Pp. iv, 258.

311. Hen, Ferdinand J. de. *Beitrag zur Kenntnis der Musikinstrumente aus Belgisch Kongo und Ruanda-Urundi.* Cologne (phil.), 1958. *Pub.*: Tervuren, 1960. Pp. 259, bibliog., illus., maps. 30 pp. "Resumé" in French.
      The author examined some 5,900 instruments.

312. Henderson, Robert V. *A Historical Study of Some Symbols Used for Notating Musical Pitch.* San Diego S. C., M.A. (music), 1962.

313. Henkin, Robert. *The Prediction of Behavioral Response Patterns to Music.* California (Los Angeles), Ph.D. (music), 1956. Pp. 323.

314. Henschel, Hildegard. *Das volkstümliche deutsche Tanzlied der neueren Zeit in seiner Beziehung zu Tanz und Musik.* Munich (phil.), 1938. Pp. 102.

315. Herreid, Henry Benjamin. *Folk Music in the United States.* Wisconsin, M.A. (music), 1938. Pp. 96, music.
      Includes chapters and sections dealing with the definition of folk music, present status of folk music in the United States, and the use of folk music. Brief discussions of Indian music, songs of the Southern Uplands, Mississippi, Afro-American songs, chanteys, war songs, songs of the shanty boy, Spanish-American songs, and cowboy and hobo songs.

41

316. Herriman, Marion E. *Latin American Music for Use in Junior High School.* Eastman, M.M., 1943.

317. Herzog, George. *A Comparison of Pueblo and Pima Musical Styles.* Columbia U., Ph.D. (anthro.), 1937. Pp. i, 134, bibliog., lists of Pueblo dances and songs, music, phonetic key, texts, vita. *Pub.: J. of Amer. Folkl.* 49 (1936), pp. 293-340, text; 341-415, music.

> Describes comparative method, Pueblo and Pima styles, vocal techniques, tonality, rhythm, structure, types, with commentary on texts, and summary.

318. Hess, Ralph Edward. *Arizona Indian Music and Suggestions for Its Use in the Elementary Schools.* So. California, M.M., 1950. Pp. 145.

> Outline of the history and culture of the major Arizona tribes based on secondary sources and regional museums. One previously unpublished transcription on page 88 of a Navaho lullaby.

319. Heth, Edward L. *The Southern Mountain Folk Songs and Their Arrangement for Unaccompanied Singing.* Westminster Choir Coll., M.A. (music), 1940. Pp. 153.

320. Hickerson, Joseph. *Annotated Bibliography of North American Indian Music North of Mexico.* Indiana U., M.A., 1961. Pp. ix, 464.

> About 1300 items. Includes a tribal index and a history of the investigation of North American Indian music.

321. Higgins, John C. *The Lumberjack in American Literature: His Life and Customs, His Slang, His Ballads and Shanties, and His Folk-Epic of Paul Bunyan.* So. California, M.A., 1935. Pp. 147, bibliog.

> Based on personal experience in northern U.S. and eastern Canada, with occasional supplements from books and periodicals.

322. Hildebrandt, Hans Ulrich. *Der Arbeitsvertrag des Musikers.* Berlin (law), 1933. *Pub.:* Berlin, Schweitzer, 1934. Pp. 99.

323. Hill, Double E. *A Study of Tastes in American Church Music as Reflected in the Music of the Methodist Episcopal Church to 1900.* Illinois, Ph.D. (music), 1962. Pp. 900. *D.A.* XXIII, 4377.

> Examination of the incipits of the tunes, and the prefaces and introductions to hymn and tunebooks and other contemporary

writings were used to determine historical backgrounds, the ideals and beliefs of John Wesley, the beginnings of Methodist hymnody in America, the camp-meeting movement, and the demand for a more "popular" type of tune.

324. Hillis, Mary Carroll. *A Study of the Origin of Certain European Folk Dances and Singing Games.* Iowa, M.A. (phy. ed.), 1940. Pp. 186.

325. Hirsch, Selma. *Studien zum Antwerpener Liederbuch vom Jahre 1544 mit einem Anhang über das Volkslied vom Grafen Friedrich.* Tübingen (phil.), 1923. Pp. vii, 332.

326. Hirt, Charles C. *Graeco-Slavonic Chant Traditions Evident in the Part-Writing of the Russian Orthodox Church.* So. California, Ph.D. (music), 1946. Pp. 461.

327. Hjortsvang, Carl T. *Scandinavian Contributions to American Sacred Music.* Union Theol. Sem., D.S.M., 1951. Pp. 255.

328. Hoehn, Eleanor J. *Popular Sheet Music in the Public Library.* Western Reserve U., M.S. (lib. sci.), 1950. Pp. 19, appendixes, bibliog.
    Based upon 22 questionnaires sent to cities with populations ranging from 100,000 to 900,000, the problem was "to discover to what extent popular music was being used in these libraries."

329. Hoerburger, Felix. *Musik aus Ungoni (Ostafrika).* Munich (phil.), 1941. Pp. 144.

330. Hoerburger, Felix. *Tanz und Tanzmusik im Bereich der albaner Jugoslaviens, unter besonderer Berucksichtigung der Musik auf Schalmei und Trommel.* Erlangen-Nuremberg (HabSchr.), 1963.

331. Hohmann, Rupert Karl. *The Church Music of the Old Order Amish of the United States.* Northwestern U., Ph.D. (music), 1959. Pp. 262, bibliog., music. *D.A.* XX, 3769.
    Deals with the history, description, illustration and stylistic analysis of hymns and other tunes taken from literary sources and phonograph recordings.

332. Holcombe, Julia Irene. *Southern Mountain Folk Songs for American Schools.* Eastman, M.M. (music ed.), 1941. Pp. vi, 108, music.
    Following a discussion of the nature of folksongs and ballads in

general, the author gives a history of the Southern Mountain folksongs, including the characteristics of the songs. Thirty-one representative songs are selected and given in notation, together with teaching suggestions. Finally, the author justifies the teaching of native folksongs in the American schools.

333. Honsel, Helen Hope. *Parallelisms in the English and German Romantic Folk-Song Revival.* Minnesota, Ph.D. (germ. lang. and lit.), 1936. Pp. ii, 198, bibliog.

Deals, in the main, with texts.

334. Hood, Mantle. *The Nuclear Theme as a Determinant of Patet in Javanese Music.* Amsterdam, Ph.D., 1954. *Pub.*: Groningen, J. B. Wolters, 1954. Pp. xi, 323, illus., transcriptions.

335. Hopps, Gloria Lorraine. *Mission Music of California.* Northwestern U., M.M., 1949.

336. Horacek, Leo. *The Relation of Mood and Melodic Pattern in Folk Songs.* Kansas, Ph.D. (music), 1955. Pp. 141. *D.A.* XVII, 1567.

Modality, melodic pattern and rhythmic structure of about 100 folksongs each of four cultures—German, French, English, and Southern Appalachian—were studied. It was concluded that melodic pattern is functional in the determining of mood expressed in the songs.

337. Horie, M. *Rhythm in African Music.* Tokyo U. Arts, 1959.

338. Hornburg, Friedrich. *Die Musik der Tiv. Ein Beitrag zur Erforschung der Musik Nigeriens.* Berlin (phil.), 1940. Summary in *Die Musikforschung* 1 (1948), pp. 47-59.

339. Howe, Winifred B. *A Comparative Study of Selected Ballad Tune Variants of the Present Day.* California (Berkeley), M.A. (music), 1941. Pp. 79 text, 15 pp. tables, 4 pp. bibliog.

A study of English and American folksongs essentially elaborating and repeating Cecil Sharp's work. Texts of the English and Scottish songs are given, followed by similar American versions.

340. Hoyt, Charles A. *Jazz and Its Origin.* Wesleyan U., B.A. (Distinction Thesis), 1953. Pp. 105, music.

A brief history of jazz with special attention to its masters, the thesis also includes a section on African music, a section on present-day trends, and a long set of indexes of selected records and bibliographies.

341. Hsiao, Yiu-mei Chopin. *Eine geschichtliche Untersuchung über das chinesische Orchester bis zum 17. Jahrhundert.* Leipzig (phil.), 1919.

342. Huber, Kurt. *Der Ausdruck musikalischer Elementarmotive. Eine experimentalpsychologische Untersuchung.* Munich (Hab-Schr.), 1919. *Pub.*: Leipzig, Barth, 1923. Pp. v, 234.

343. Huchzermeyer, Helmut. *Aulos u. Kithara in der griechischen Musik bis zum Ausgang der klassischen Zeit (nach den literarischen Quellen).* Münster (phil.), 1931. Pp. 76.

344. Hudson, Arthur Palmer. *Folk-Songs of Mississippi and Their Background: A Study, with Texts.* North Carolina, Ph.D. (engl.), 1930. Bibliog., title and first-line indexes of songs. *Pub.*: Chapel Hill, Univ. of No. Car. Press, 1936. Pp. xii, 321, bibliog., no music.
> In order to indicate their relation to the lives, character and interests of the people of Mississippi, their connections with Old World traditions and with indigenous American culture, and their qualities as folk literature, 156 selected ballads and songs (207 texts), recovered by the editor and others from oral circulation among white people of Mississippi, were studied.

345. Hübner, Herbert. *Die Musik im Bismarck-Archipel. Musikethnologische Studien zur Kulturkreislehre und Rassenforschung.* Jena (phil.), 1936 (1938). *Pub.*: Schriften z. Volksliedkunde u. völkerkundl. Musikwiss. 1 (Berlin, Hahnefeld, 1938). Pp. vi, 117.

346. Huebner, Richard Alden. *A Practical Study of 67 Lieder . . . and 132 Volkslieder Settings . . . by Ludwig van Beethoven.* Wayne State U., M.A. (music), 1960. Pp. 187, bibliog., tables.
> Includes brief studies of folksongs as arranged by Beethoven and some statements on the sources of the tunes.

347. Hüttel, Walter Oskar. *Zur Geschichte des deutschen Volksliedes im 17. Jahrhundert.* Berlin, H.U. (phil.), 1957. Pp. v, 207, diagrs.; pp. 208-405, music.

348. Hummel, Lynn Ellis. *Ozark Folk-songs.* Missouri, M.A. (music), 1936. Pp. 217, bibliog., music.
> More than 250 Ozark folksongs are listed in three categories: ballads brought from the British Isles, songs of more recent times, and songs for special occasions. Characteristics are analyzed according to keys, pitches, slur notes, and rhythm. Material gathered in the field.

349. Hummel, Lynn Ellis. *The Music Experiences and Attitudes of Rural Children in Northeast Missouri.* Missouri, Ed.D., 1950. Pp. 267. *D.A.* X, no. 4, p. 107.

> 1,544 children from grades one to eight, in 107 rural schools, were studied in an attempt to discover the nature of the activities and the experiences of the children in the use of music, the things which rural children do in their daily living that have some aspect of music about them, and what experiences children would like to have with music.

350. Huston, James Stafford. *Greek Folk Music for the Elementary and Junior High Schools.* Ohio State U., M.A. (music), 1940.

351. Huth, Arno. *Die Musikinstrumente Ost-Turkistans bis zum 11. Jahrhundert n. Chr.* Berlin (phil.), 1928. Pp. 53.

352. Imbescheid, Ernst. *Die Melodien der Volkslieder in Oberhessen.* Giessen (phil.), 1941. Pp. 122.

353. Irving, Sydney Edward. *East Indian Music.* Redlands, M.A. (music), 1941. Pp. 54.

354. Isbell, Sarah Rachel. *Musical Talent of Indians.* Denver, M.A. (educ.), 1928. Pp. 81.

> Data gathered at the Chilocco Indian Agricultural School, Chilocco, Oklahoma. Tests given in pitch, memory, intensity, consonance, and rhythm. The findings indicate: in pitch and memory, Indians were inferior to whites; in intensity and consonance, equal; in rhythm, slightly better; in time, boys are better than whites, but girls somewhat inferior.

355. Ives, Edward Dawson. *The Satirical Song Tradition in Maine and the Maritime Provinces of Canada, with Particular Reference to Larry Gorman.* Indiana U., Ph.D. (folkl.), 1962. Pp. 470, bibliog., maps, music. *D.A.* XXIII, 1655. *Pub.: Larry Gorman; the Man Who Made the Songs* (Bloomington, Indiana U.P., 1964). Pp. xv, 225.

> References to 79 songs, 21 of which are given with their tunes, of "the most famous creator of traditional songs in the Northeast."

356. Izikowitz, Karl Gustav. *Musical and Other Sound Instruments of the South American Indians; A Comparative Ethnographical Study.* Göteborgs Högskola (phil.), 1935. *Pub.:* Göteborgs

Kungl. Vetenskaps- och Vitterhets-Samhälles. *Handlingar,* series 5A, vol. 5, no. 1 (Göteborg, 1935). Pp. xii, 433, bibliog., diagrs., photos, tables.

> Discussion of the history, technical details, uses and distribution of individual instruments classified into the traditional subdivisions: Idiophones, Membranophones, Chordophones and Aerophones.

357. Jackson, Beulah Mary. *The Rise and Development of Harvest Customs and Festivals.* Geo. Peabody, M.A., 1933. Pp. 78.

> Brief consideration of early Creek festivals, and North American Indian Corn Dances in general.

358. Jackson, Eileen Stanza. *The Use of Negro Folk Song in Symphonic Forms.* Chicago, M.A. (music), 1941. Pp. 42.

359. Jacobson, Olga J. *The Influence of Traditional Norwegian Folk Music Upon Grieg's Violin Sonata, opus 13, no. 2.* Iowa, M.A. (music), 1931.

360. Jenkins, Mildred Leona. *The Impact of African Music Upon the Western Hemisphere.* Boston U., M.A., 1942. Pp. 60, illus., music.

> Reaches the conclusion that the impact of African music on the Western Hemisphere has resulted in new, and quasi-native musics. Chapters deal with African music, its structure, African elements in American music, white spirituals, jazz, and the influence of African upon Latin American music.

361. Jenkins, Ruth Elizabeth. *An Historical Study of the Dances of the Mexican Indians in the Latter Pre-Hispanic Colonial and Modern Periods of Mexico.* New York U., M.A. (phy. ed.), 1932. Pp. 41.

362. Johnson, Ella Victoria. *Form in Exotic Music.* Cornell U., M.A. (music), 1926.

363. Johnson, Ellen Louise. *The Unpublished Mountain Folk Songs Collected by Dorothy Scarborough.* Baylor U., M.A. (engl.), 1941. 2 vols. Pp. 736.

364. Johnson, Florence Booco. *A Comparative Study of the Basic Music Talents of Three Racial Groups—Chinese, Japanese, and Part Hawaiian.* Hawaii, M.A., 1933. Pp. 95.

> Oriented around the Seashore tests, the author tested 300 high school students, from ages 14 to 20, for pitch, intensity, time,

consonance, tonal memory, and rhythm. From these six tests it was concluded that age as a factor plays no part in musical capacities, and that the Hawaiians showed the greatest musical capacity of the three groups tested.

365. Johnson, Guy Benton. *A Study of the Musical Talent of the American Negro.* North Carolina, Ph.D. (sociol.), 1927.

3500 Negroes in the schools of North Carolina, South Carolina and Virginia were given a series of tests devised and standardized by Seashore in an attempt to measure the difference, if any, between the natural musical endowments of the white people and Negroes. No appreciable differences were found after the use of these tests which bear only upon the passive or sensitivity phases—not the motor phases, which may be significant—of musical talent.

366. Johnson, James Winfred. *The Status and Administration of Student Dance Bands in Colleges and Universities in the United States.* North Texas S.T.C., M.A. (music), 1947.

367. Johnson, Marie S. *Mexican Folk-lore.* Northwestern U., M.M., 1943. Pp. 114, bibliog., 10 music exs.

Deals with music, dance, literature, drama, in terms of the eras of the Aztecs; Spanish Colonization; renascence and nationalism. Also includes a brief history of Mexico and a supplement with words of *corrido*.

368. Johnson, Marlowe W. *The Musical Nationalism of Carlos Chavez and Other Twentieth-Century Mexican Composers, with Special Regard to the Use of Indigenous Materials.* Indiana U., Ph.D. (music theory). In process.

369. Johnston, Edith Louise. *The Use of Mexican Folk Dances in School Activities.* Texas, M.A. (phy. ed.), 1937.

370. Jones, Carrie Roberta. *Supplementary and Background Material for the Teaching of Folk Dances.* Iowa, M.A. (phy. ed.), 1944.

371. Jones, Henry Broadus. *The Death Song of the "Noble Savage": A Study in the Idealization of the American Indian.* Chicago, Ph.D., 1924. Pp. 144.

Mostly North American, but considers South and Central America. Historical essay on early writers and the death song.

372. Jones, John Alan. *The Role of the Sun Dance in Northern Ute Acculturation.* Columbia U., Ph.D. (anthro.), 1950. Pp. 104, bibliog., map. *D.A.* XI, 454.

> Sun Dance discussed as the focal point of Northern Ute culture; identification of Ute bands, culture history; functional analysis of the Sun Dance.

373. Jones, Trevor Alan. *An Introductory Survey of the Aboriginal Music of Arnhem Land.* Sydney, B.A., Honours, First Class (music), 1953. Pp. 104, map, music, photos.

> A preliminary study which is largely unreliable in comparison to the author's M.A. thesis which follows.

374. Jones, Trevor Alan. *Arnhem Land Music (North Australia).* Sydney, M.A. Honours, First Class (music), 1958. Pp. 174, 174 music exs., 30 full transcriptions. *Pub.: Oceania Monograph* 9 (University of Sydney, 1958).

> A large-scale survey which includes detailed description and music analysis.

375. Jones, Trevor Alan. *The Didjeridu: An Ethnomusicological Study of the Techniques and Function of the Australian Aboriginal Wooden Trumpet and Related Instruments Throughout the World.* Sydney, Ph.D. In process.

376. Jorgensen, Sigurd. *The Danish Folk High School with Emphasis upon the "Living Word," Folk Song, and Gymnastics.* Ohio State U., Ph.D. (educ.), 1945.

> A unique experiment in private education begun in 1844 in which hymns and folksongs play an important part.

377. Jurk, Ingeborg. *Volkstümliche Lärminstrumente.* Hamburg (phil.), 1937. Pp. ii, 157; appendix, 66 pp., illus. *Pub.*: (as by Ingeborg Jurk-Bauer) Quakenbrück, C. Trute, 1937. Pp. vii, 52, illus.

378. Kaap, Theodore F., Jr. *A Survey of the Teaching of Music in Indian Schools of the Southwest with Suggestions for Improvement of Such Instruction.* Arizona, M.A., 1951. Pp. 94.

> As a result of 125 replies to questionnaires, author finds some music taught where facilities are available. Music instruction needs supervision and standardization, more texts and musical instruments. There is also need for in-service training and a course of study.

379. Kanda, S. *Classification of Pentatonic Scales.* Tokyo U. Arts, 1959.

380. Kaplan, Arthur Abraham. *Popular Music as a Reflection of the Depression Era.* So. California, M.A. (music), 1949. Pp. 199, music.

Relates texts and music to spiritual values of the people as affected by socio-economic conditions.

381. Kaplan, Max. *The Musician in America: A Study of His Social Roles. Introduction to a Sociology of Music.* Illinois, Ph.D. (sociol.), 1951. Pp. 445, bibliog., table. *D.A.* XII, 110.

The dissertation is divided into three sections "which constitute the base for a sociology of music": functions of music, major social patterns in which music is to be found, social roles of musicians.

382. Karklin, Jutta. *Deutsche Volksliedmotive im Liederschatz der Letten und Litauer.* Heidelberg (phil.), 1955. Pp. 198.

383. Karlinger, Felix. *Beiträge zu einer Volkskunde der Pyrenäen im Spiegel der Volkslieder.* Munich (phil.), 1948 (1949). Pp. 204.

384. Katner, Wilhelm. *Musik und Medizin im Zeitalter des Barock.* Leipzig (med.), 1950. Pp. 56.

385. Kaufmann, Howard Keva. *Cheyenne Indian Music and its Cultural Background.* Indiana U., A.M. (anthro.), 1952. Pp. iv, 312, bibliog., 54 musical exs., 54 contour charts, 3 charts, 6 appendixes, record list according to Indiana Univ. Archives of Traditional Music.

Discusses the history, ethnography, and aesthetics of Cheyenne dances, songs, and musical instruments.

386. Kay, Marjorie Lew. *Augmenting Oriental Dance Movement by the Adaptation of Modern Dance Techniques.* Wellesley C., M.S. (phy. ed.), 1942. Pp. 103.

387. Kealiinohomoku, Joann Wheeler. *A Comparative Study of Dance as a Constellation of Motor Behaviors Among African and United States Negroes.* Northwestern U., M.A. (anthro.), 1965. Pp. v, 170, bibliog., charts, dance notations.

This study suggests a methodology for the analysis of dance behavior by setting up taxonomies, charts for showing quantitative distribution of behavior traits, and by the use of the Kurath notation system. With the analysis of over one hundred notations, the writer shows a close, positive comparison of African and United States Negro dance behaviors. The conclusion is reënforced by an analysis of contrasting dance behaviors of Scottish and Irish dance.

338. Keefe, Mildred Jones. *Carols; Their Origin in and Connection with Dramatic Ritual and Folkways.* Boston U., M.A., 1936. Pp. vii, 101, bibliog., music.

389. Keen, James A. *Some Musical Aspects of the Moravian Church, Including the Easter Service at Winston-Salem, N.C.* Iowa, M.A. (music), 1935.

390. Keh, Chung Sik. *Die koreanische Musik. Einführung und Besprechung von 17 zum erstenmal in die europäische Notenschrift übertragenen Kompositionen.* Basel (phil.), 1934. *Pub.: Sammlung musikwiss. Abhandlungen* 17 (Strassburg, Heintz, 1934). Pp. iv, 77, 16.

391. Kemlein, Magdalene. *Die musikalische Improvisation in ihren gegenwärtigen Erscheinungsformen und als Mittel der Schulmusikerziehung.* Berlin, H.U. (educ.), 1956 (1957). Pp. iii, 193, vi.

392. Kenefick, Ruth Maureen. *The Power and Position of the Spanish and Mexican Folk Dance in Southern California.* Claremont C., M.A. (phy. ed.), 1936. Pp. 69.

393. Kern, Charlotte Helen. *Music in the Education of Primitive Racial Groups.* Washington, M.A. (music), 1934. Pp. 136.

394. Kerner, Corinne Minna. *The Music of India.* Northwestern U., M.M., 1942. Pp. 82, bibliog., music.
Deals primarily with Hindustani music, including such chapters as history, early composers, drums and the art of drumming, *tala, raga,* grace notes, instruments. Bibliography annotated.

395. Kerr, Thomas Henderson. *A Critical Survey of Printed Vocal Arrangements of Afro-American Religious Folk Songs.* Eastman, M.M. (music theory), 1939. Pp. vi, 130, music.
Concerned primarily with the history of the Afro-American religious folksong. A number of songs are given in notation and discussed from the point of view of scale and stylistic methods.

396. Kestin, Diane. *Folklore in Published and Unpublished American Opera of the Twentieth Century.* California (Los Angeles), M.A. (music), 1955. Pp. 370, bibliog.
Traces folk themes and folk music as treated in American opera.

397. Khatschi, Khatschi. *Der Dastgah. Studien zur neuen persischen Musik.* Cologne (phil.), 1960. *Pub.: Kölner Beiträge zur Musikforschung* 19 (Regensburg, Gustav Bosse Verl., 1962). Pp. 159, music.

398. Kida, M. *Musical Instruments in Ancient Central Asia.* Tokyo U. Arts, 1959.

399. Kidder, Eva G. *A Study of Latin American Music.* Illinois Wesleyan U., M.A. (music), 1943.

400. Kilpatrick, Jack Frederick. *The Possible Relationship of Content to Form in Certain Gros Ventre Songs.* Catholic U., M.A. (music), 1946. Pp. 46, music, tables.
Nine songs were selected and transcribed from a group of 116 recorded during an expedition to the Gros Ventre tribe of Montana under the auspices of the Department of Anthropology of the Catholic Univ. of America. The author attempted to determine if there was a relationship in the musical structure of the songs analyzed. There is a relationship proven but it is slight.

401. Kim, Soon Ae. *Traditional Musical Instruments and Folk Songs of Korea.* Eastman, M.M. (music theory), 1956. Pp. iv, 95, diagrs., maps, music, photos, tables.
A short history of Korean music, with dates or eras in which traditional instruments were introduced, together with descriptions and pictures showing salient features of each. Some attention paid to scales, tuning, etc. Discussion of songs confined to the most popular of the folksongs.

402. King, Bernice Margaret. *A Study of Form and Expression in American Indian Music as Exemplified in the Songs of Jemez Pueblo.* Minnesota, M.A. (anthro.), 1935. Pp. 270, bibliog., illus., music, photos.
As a result of seminar studies at the University of New Mexico Field School at Jemez Springs, New Mexico, and field work with the nearby Jemez Indians in 1931-1933, the author presents a description and analysis of 70 songs. Tables show specific occurrences of certain types of song structure, interval patterns, rhythms, modulations, progressions and other features.

403. King, Dearine E. *A Comparative Study of a Group of Standard Hymns and Gospel Songs.* Howard U., M.A. (relig. ed.), 1940. Pp. 108.

404. Kinney, Sylvia. *A Transcription and Analysis of Six Bulu Songs From the Cameroons.* Wayne State U., (essay) (music), 1961. Pp. 53, bibliog., music.

    Based on songs from a Folkways record.

405. Kinscella, Hazel Gertrude. *Songs of the American Negro and Their Influence Upon Composed Music.* Columbia U., M.A. (music), 1934. Pp. ii, 43, 60 tables.

    From the introduction: "This study of Negro song is undertaken for the purpose of defining the true characteristics of it as it now stands, and to show how it may profitably be used as an inspirational source for the creation of composed art music."

406. Kircher, Erwin. *Volkslied und Volkspoesie in der Sturmund Drangzeit.* Freiburg i. Br. (phil.), 1902. *Pub.: Zeitschrift für deutsche Wortforschung* 4 (1902).

407. Kirn, H. *The Sources and Stylistic Development of Israeli Music Since 1930.* Trinity Coll. of Music, Ph.D., 1961.

408. Kirschner, Heinrich. *Beiträge zum deutschen Volkslied-Stil um 1500.* Cologne (phil.), 1935. *Pub.: Deutsche Arbeiten der Universität Köln* 8 (Jena, Diederichs, 1935). Pp. 66.

409. Kirtley, Robert Cecil. *An Historical Study of the Japanese Noh Play A.D. 552 to 1900.* So. California, M.A. (drama), 1951. Pp. 87, illus.

410. Klein, Paul. *Volkslied und Volkstanz in Pommern.* Greifswald (phil.), 1934. *Pub.: Vorarbeiten zum Pommerschen Wörterbuch* 6 (Greifswald, Bamberg, 1935). Pp. 191.

411. Klink, Jane Seymour. *Relation of the Medicine Man to the Educational System of the Early Races of North America.* Chicago, A.M. (sociol.), 1902. Pp. 50, drawings.

    In a general study of the functions of the medicine man and his relations to the people of the tribe, some mention is made of his function as teacher of ceremonial songs and dance.

53

412. Klusen, Ernst. *Das Volkslied im niederrheinischen Dorf. Studien zum Liedgut der Gemeinde Hinsbeck.* Bonn (phil.), 1941. *Pub.*: *Veröff. des Niederrheinischen Volksliedarchivs Viersen. Wissenschaftliche Reihe* 1 (Potsdam, Voggenreiter, 1941). Pp. 99.

413. Knox, Winifred I. *Folksongs from the Olympic Peninsula and Puget Sound.* Juilliard, M.A. (music), 1945. Pp. 96.

414. Knudson, Emma R. *Folk Music as a Tool in Intercultural Education.* Northwestern U., Ph.D. (educ.), 1946. Pp. 390.
    Investigates type and extent and selects, classifies and arranges 1198 folksongs from 84 countries, including 226 from the U.S., 146 from England, 114 from France, 96 from Germany, 65 from various Latin American countries and 62 from Russia, for use in elementary schools.

415. Kolesch, Hermann. *Schwabentum im Schwabenlied.* Tübingen (phil.), 1937. *Pub.*: *Arbeiten aus d. Inst. für dt. Volkskunde* 1 (Stuttgart, Kohlhammer, 1937). Pp. 169.

416. Kolinski, Mieczyslaw. *Die Musik der Primitivstämme auf Malaka und ihre Beziehungen zur samoanischen Musik.* Berlin (phil.), 1930. *Pub.*: *Anthropos* 25 (1930), pp. 585-648.

417. Koller, Ernst. *Musse und Musiche Paideia. Über die Musikaporetik in der aristotelischen Politik.* Zurich (phil.), 1956. *Pub.*: Basel, B. Schwabe, 1956. Pp. 68. Also *Museum Helveticum* 13 (1956), pp. 1-37, 94-124.
    A discussion of the role of music as an ethical force in the Greek city-state as expressed by Aristotle and Plato.

418. Kolneder, Walter. *Die vokale Mehrstimmigkeit in der Volksmusik der österreichischen Alpenländer.* Innsbruck (phil.), 1949. Pp. 163.

419. Kovačević, Krešimir. *Das kroatische Volkslied aus dem Murinselgebiet.* Leipzig (phil.), 1943. Pp. 148.

420. Kovach, James Emery. *Songs of the Magyars.* Ohio State U., M.A. (music), 1940.

421. Krader, Barbara Lattimer. *Serbian Peasant Wedding Songs: A Formal, Semantic and Functional Analysis.* Radcliffe C., Ph.D., 1955. 2 vols. Pp. 675, bibliog., no music.
    Description and analysis of texts (not quoted) to about 1000

songs, collected over the past 150 years from Vojvodina, Serbia, Montenegro, Bosnia and Herzegovina, Kosovo-Metoliya, and Serbian ethnic groups in Macedonia. Accounts of wedding ritual and general description of music involved.

422. Kramolisch, Walter. *Studien zur musikalischen Gestalt des epischen Liedes in Bulgarien.* Prague (phil.), 1938.

423. Krauss, Paul G. *Loblied; German Secular Song of Praise, 1450-1650.* Illinois, Ph.D. (germ. lit.), 1937.

424. Krehbiel, James W. *Rhythm, Meter and Syncopation.* Indiana U., M.M., 1958. Pp. viii, 79, bibliog., music.
Discusses the difference between rhythm and meter in music (each treated historically with definitions), the psychological aspects of meter and rhythm, and the "principal object of the thesis," syncopation.

425. Kreidler, Walter. *Die volkstümlichen Tanzmusikkapellen des deutschen Sprachgebietes.* Frankfurt a.M. (HabSchr.), 1941.

426. Krupsky, Dhannon Harry. *Singing Americana: A Study of Democracy in Song.* DePaul U., M.M.Ed., 1943. Pp. 169.

427. Kündig, Alice. *Das Musikerlebnis in psychologischer und psychotherapeutischer Sicht mit besonderer Berucksichtigung seiner kompensatorischen Funktion.* Zürich (phil.), 1960. *Pub.*: Winterthur, Keller, 1961. Pp. xii, 108.

428. Künzig, Johann. *Das Volkslied in Baden einst und getzt. T. 1: Geschichte des Volksliedinteresses in Baden.* Heidelberg (phil.), 1922. Pp. vi, 128. Summary in *Jahrb. d. Phil. Fak. Heidelberg* 1921/22, part 1, pp. 46-49.

429. Kürth, Brigitte. *Das deutsche Kinderlied des 19. Jahrhunderts.* Halle (phil.), 1955. Pp. 117, xxxv; 154 xxi; iv, 147.

430. Kuh, Koh-nie. *A Musicological Study of the Important Tonal Systems of the T'ang Dynasty (A.D. 618-907).* New York U., Ed.D. (music ed.), 1942. Pp. 271.

431. Kunert, Ernst. *Die Entwicklung der formalistischen Musikästhetik im Altertum.* Leipzig (phil.), 1924. Pp. ii, 118.

432. Kurokawa, T. *Rhythm of Noh Play Music.* Tokyo U. Arts, 1958.

433. Laade, Wolfgang. *Die Struktur des korsischen Lamento-Melodik.* Berlin, F.U. (phil.), 1960. *Pub.: Sammlung Musikwiss. Abhandlungen* 43 (Strasbourg, P. H. Heitz, 1962). Pp. 126, 101 music exs., 12 tables.

434. Lachmann, Robert. *Die Musik in den tunisischen Städten.* Berlin (phil.), 1922. *Pub.: AfMw* 5 (1923), pp. 136-170.

435. LaGala, Stella S. *Selected Polish Songs and Dances.* (score) Northwestern U., M.M., 1949.

436. Lambert, E. Elizabeth. *A Survey of Music in Negro Colleges and Universities.* New Eng. Conserv. of Music, B.A. (music), 1945.

437. Lamont, Herbert Barry. *A Study of the Folk Song Variations in the Music of the English Virginal Composers.* So. California, A.M. (music), 1952. Pp. 160, music.
    Discusses the technique of variation rather than the origin of the melodies.

438. Lamson, Roy, Jr. *English Broadside Ballad Tunes.* Harvard, Ph.D., 1936.

439. Lamson, Sophie Mollie. *Music and Culture in the Caribbean.* Wesleyan U., M.A., 1957. Pp. iv, 156, bibliog., music.
    The result of a two-months' study on St. John in the Virgin Islands, the thesis attempts to relate calypso songs sung by members of the St. John community to West Indian culture.

440. Landels, J. G. *Ancient Greek Musical Instruments of the Woodwind Family.* Hull, Ph.D., 1961.

441. Lantis, Margaret. *Alaskan Eskimo Ceremonialism.* California, Ph.D. (anthro.), 1939.

442. LaRue, Adrian Jan Pieter. *The Okinawan Classical Songs; An Analytical and Comparative Study.* Harvard, Ph.D. (music), 1952. Pp. 260, bibliog., 155 musical exs., 15 plates, and 17 pp. complete musical pieces.
    The study summarizes the culture and history of Okinawa briefly, continuing with chapters on the musical instruments, vocal style and notation system. The songs are examined with respect to form, texts, melody, rhythm, heterophony and relationships with Chinese and Japanese music. A microfilm of transcriptions of the entire Okinawan repertory is on deposit with the dissertation.

443. Laufer, Robin. *Der polnische Tanz und sein Eindringen in die Kunstmusik.* Vienna (phil.), 1935. *Pub.*: Lemberg, A. Bodek, 1936 (Polish translation).

444. Laws, George Malcolm, Jr. *Native American Balladry; A Descriptive Study and a Bibliographical Syllabus of the Ballads Sung in the United States.* Pennsylvania, Ph.D. (engl. lit.), 1949. *Pub.*: Amer. Folklore Soc., *Pubs.*, Bibl. Ser., vol. 1 (Philadelphia, 1950). Pp. xii, 276, bibliog., index to ballads discussed, tables, no music.
>   The "Descriptive Study" (pp. 1-112) includes discussions of American ballad forms, variants and types, illustrated by texts. The "Bibliographical Syllabus" is a series of appendixes of which the first is a bibliography of 185 native ballads in oral tradition which are grouped into nine subject categories, war, cowboy and pioneer, lumberjack, sailor, Negro, and others, giving a short summary of each ballad with a sample stanza.

445. Laycock, Harold R. *A History of Music in the Academies of the Latter-Day Saints Church, 1876-1926.* So. California, D.M.A., 1961. Pp. 521. *D.A.* XXII, 1656.
>   Attempts to develop a comprehensive picture of the practices of music education and music performance in the Academies.

446. Lazaro, Felicidad M. *A Collection of Unpublished Dances of the Philippines.* Springfield C., M.A., 1955. Pp. 62.

447. Lehmann, Günther. *Theorie und Geschichte der griechischen Harmonik der Darstellung durch August Boeckh.* Hamburg (phil.), 1934 (1935). *Pub.*: Würzburg, R. Mayr, 1935. Pp. lvii, 112, diagrs., illus., music, tables.
>   The first part is a discussion, the second part a translation of A. Boeckh's "Harmonik der Griechen" (*De metris Pindari*, Book III, chapters 7-12).

448. Lekis, Lisa. *The Origin and Development of Ethnic Caribbean Dance and Music.* Florida, Ph.D., 1956. Pp. 294, bibliog. *D.A.* XVI, 1126.
>   Broad treatment of the role of the aboriginal Indians, Afro-Caribbeans and Europeans.

449. Lembo, Frank Ralph. *American War Songs.* Coll.-Conserv. of Music of Cincinnati, M.M., 1947. Pp. 164, bibliog., appendix.
>   Compilation of texts of songs from various wars, also listing familiar tunes to which some of the texts were sung, the history of the text and a source where the song may be found.

450. LeMon, Melvin William. *Pennsylvania Anthracite Miners' Folksongs.* Eastman, Ph.D. (music), 1941. 2 vols., plus 15 phono records, illus., music.

> A study of the folksongs, as well as recordings.

451. Lentschner, Sofie. *The Four Hymns Appended to the Passover Haggadah of the German Jews.* New York U., M.A. (music), 1939.

452. Leskinen, V. O. *Finnish Folk Music Suitable for Use in the American Classroom.* So. California, M.M., 1947. Pp. 167, music.

> Includes characteristics of Finnish music and examples from Finnish collections. Finnish sources and records also used.

453. Lester, Lotus Alene. *The Effect of the Social, Political and Religious Conditions Upon Music.* DePaul U., M.M.Ed., 1940. Pp. 90.

454. Lewis, Arthur Ansel. *American Songsters, 1800-1805.* Brown U., M.A. (engl.), 1937. Pp. 306.

> A continuation of the Alice Louise Thorpe thesis. See under this name for annotation.

455. Lewis, Madalynne Solomon. *Some Mexican Folk Dances as Found in Los Angeles, California: Music, Choreographies, and Photographs.* California (Los Angeles), M.A. (phy. ed.), 1941.

456. Ley, Margaret. *Spirituals. Ein Beitrag zur Analyse der religiösen Liedschöpfung bei der nordamerikanischen Negern in der Zeit der Sklaverei.* Munich (phil.), 1954. Pp. 85.

457. Lichtheim, Miriam. *Songs of the Harpers.* Chicago, Ph.D., 1944. Pp. 93. *Pub.:* (in part) *J. of Near Eastern Studies* 4 (1945), pp. 178-212. "Bibliog. of Harpers' Songs from Monuments of the New Kingdom"; plates of inscriptions of songs in copy and photographs.

> A general discussion of "harpers' songs" and "orchestra songs" as well as discussions of over ten specific songs recorded either on monuments or papyri of ancient Egypt.

458. Lieberman, Fredric. *Contemporary Japanese Composition: Its Relationship to Concepts of Traditional Oriental Musics.* Hawaii, M.A. (music), 1965. Pp. vii, 161.

> A study of compositions by Ichiyanagi, Mayazumi and Takemitsu in the light of traditional oriental aesthetics.

459. Liebstoekl, Friedrich. *Das deutsche Vaudeville. Ein Beitrag zur Geschichte des deutschen Dramas und Theaters.* Vienna (phil.), 1923. Pp. 66.

460. Lincoln, Martha Louise. *The Cherokee Outlet and Its Music.* So. California, M.M., 1949. Pp. 117, maps, music.
   Based on experiences while teaching school, the thesis concentrates on cowboy and settler's music and includes some original transcriptions based on 1946-1948 recordings.

461. Lindegren, Ruth Marie. *Origins of Folk Dances.* Wellesley C., M.S. (phy. ed.), 1940. Pp. 86.

462. Lindemann, Konrad. *Der Berufsstand der Unterhaltungsmusiker in Hamburg.* Hamburg (phil.), 1938 (1939). *Pub.: Volk und Gemeinschaft* 3 (Hamburg, Hansischer Gildenverl., 1938). Pp. 77.

463. Lisewski, Mary Ann. *Music in Poland.* Northwestern U., M.M., 1944. Pp. 71.

464. Litle, Velma Mary Lois. *A Study of the Significance of Three National Dance Groups in Los Angeles.* California (Los Angeles), M.A. (phy. ed.), 1943. Pp. 48, photos.
   An inquiry into the cultural significance of Swedish, Czechoslovakian, and Hungarian dance groups. Includes history, costumes, performances, and festivals.

465. Littell, William J. *A Survey of the Uses of Music in Correctional Institutions in the United States.* Kansas, M.A. (music), 1962.

466. Loessel, Earl Oliver. *The Use of Character Notes and Other Unorthodox Notations in Teaching the Reading of Music in Northern United States During the Nineteenth Century.* Michigan, Ph.D. (music), 1959. Pp. 571, bibliog., pls., tables. *D.A.* XX, 1820.
   Contains an annotated bibliography, with full citations and showing locations in libraries, of tune and hymn books.

467. Loft, Abram. *Musicians' Guild and Union: A Consideration of the Evaluation of Protective Organization Among Musicians.* Columbia U., Ph.D. (musicol.), 1950. Pp. 408.

468. Logan, Adeline Marie. *American National Music in the Compositions of Charles Ives.* Washington, M.A. (music), 1943. Pp. 77, bibliog.

A description of Charles Ives' music with short musical examples demonstrating his use of American national music, which includes patriotic songs, folk airs, country dances, prairie songs, Indian music, jazz, and hymns.

469. Long, Clayton Augustius. *The Sociological Aspects of the Windband in American Community Life.* Pacific, M.A. (music), 1947. Pp. 74.

470. Long, Norman G. *The Theology and Psychology of the Negroes' Religion Prior to 1860 as Shown Particularly in the Spirituals.* Oberlin C., M.A., 1936.

471. Lopez, Hernando Diaz. *The Moorish-Arabic Influence on Spanish Music.* New Eng. Conserv. of Music, M.A. (music), 1935. Pp. 188, vii, bibliog., illus., music.

A history of the influence exerted by the Moors and Arabs on Spanish music during the days of the Moslem occupation of the Spanish peninsula, 711-1492 A.D. Includes a brief sketch of the history of Spain, the origin and character of Moorish-Arab music and its influence upon Christian Spain and present-day Spanish music.

472. Lossing, Laverna Lucy. *A Study of the Character and Role of Music Among the California Indians.* So. California, M.A. (hist.), 1934. Pp. 71, bibliog., illus., music.

An investigation of the musical culture of California Indians, including a study of their songs and instruments.

473. Lowry, Ira Pate. *The Instrumental Music of the Indians of Robeson County, North Carolina.* Ohio State U., M.A. (music), 1942.

474. Lucas, John Samuel. *Rhythms of Negro Music and Negro Poetry.* Minnesota, M.A., 1945. Pp. 241, bibliog.

Part I deals with rhythms in music as illustrated in religious (jubilee and gospel) songs, and secular (popular, work, gang, shout, blues, jazz) songs. Part II discusses poetry, chronologically by poet, including Derivative and Dialect Poetry (1760-1900), Transitional (1900-1920), and Poetry of the New Negro (1920-1945).

475. Luke, Orral Stanford. *Differences in Musical Aptitude in School Children of Different National and Racial Origin.* California (Berkeley), Ph.D., 1939. Pp. 149.
>Includes 168 northern Europeans, 109 Italians, 130 Chinese, 55 Japanese, and 31 Spanish and Portuguese.

476. Luta, Vasile Gh. *Die deutschen Volkslieder auf Napoleon I. von seinen Anfängen bis zum Beginn der Befreiungskriege. Ein Beitrag zu ihrer Erforschung.* Berlin (phil.), 1931. Pp. 71.

477. McAdams, Nettie F. *The Folksongs of the American Negro; A Collection of Unprinted Texts Preceded by a General Survey of the Traits of the Negro Song.* California, M.A., 1923.

478. McAleer, John J. *Songs and Ballads Loyal to the Hanoverian Succession.* Harvard, Ph.D. (engl. lit.), 1955.

479. McAllester, David Park. *Peyote Music.* Columbia U., Ph.D. (anthro.), 1949. Pp. 103, bibliog., diagrs., 30 pp. music, tables, texts. *Pub.:* Viking Fund Inc., *Pubs. in Anthro.* 13 (N.Y., 1949). Pp. 104, text; pp. 62, bibliog., music, tables.
>Discusses the Peyote ceremony, texts and songs; compares the styles of fourteen tribes for similarities and differences, discusses sources of the style, and defines it.

480. Macare, Helen H. *The Singing Saints: A Study of the Mormon Hymnal, 1835-1950.* California (Los Angeles), Ph.D. (lang. and lit.), 1961.

481. McClurg, Robert Gilmore. *Semitic Music.* Oregon, M.A. (music), 1941. Pp. 477.

482. McCorkle, Donald Macomber. *An Introduction to the Musical Culture of the North Carolina Moravians in the Eighteenth Century.* Indiana U., A.M. (music), 1953. Pp. v, 112, bibliog., facsimiles, small number of musical exs. showing traditional chorale melodies and the way they appear in Moravian music.
>A description of the musical life of the Moravians in the Wachovia settlement in northwestern North Carolina from 1753 to 1800.

483. McCorkle, Donald Macomber. *Moravian Music in Salem; A German-American Heritage.* Indiana U., Ph.D. (music), 1958. Pp. 431. *D.A.* XX, 688.
>Covers all aspects of music in the period 1780-1840.

484. McCorkle, Thomas Smith. *Music in Greek Life and Some of Its Educational Implications.* So. Methodist U., M.A., 1936. Pp. 97.

485. McCullough, Edna Olivia. *A Dance Cycle Giving a Visual Representation of Rhythm, Primitive, Ancient, Medieval and Modern.* Iowa, M.A. (phy. ed.), 1933.

486. McDonald, Grant. *A Study of Selected Folk-Songs of Southern Missouri.* Iowa, M.A. (music), 1939. Pp. vii, 100.
    Includes music and texts of thirty-seven songs collected by the author in Christian, Greene, Stone and Taney counties.

487. Maceda, Corazon S. *Philippine Folk Songs in Music Education.* Eastman, M.A. (music ed.), 1948. Pp. iv, 119, illus., map, music.
    The author cites some Philippine folksongs and considers their adaptability to a program in public school music instruction. A brief sketch of the background of the songs is given.

488. Maceda, Jose. *The Music of the Magindanao.* California (Los Angeles), Ph.D. In process.

489. MacFarland, Gertrude Straight. *The Sociology of Music with Special Reference to the Rural Scene.* Kentucky, M.S. (sociol.), 1943. Pp. 111.

490. McGhee, Charles Bernard. *The Primitive Music of the Alaskan Eskimo.* Northwestern U., M.M., 1947. Pp. iv, 50, bibliog., 5 figs., 11 music exs.
    Contains chapters on the Eskimo, his songs, dances, drums, song language, and brief music analysis.

491. McHargue, Robert Morris. *Study in the Popular Music of the American Frontiers.* California (Berkeley), M.A. (hist.), 1940.

492. McIntosh, David Seneff. *Some Representative Southern Folk-Songs.* Iowa, M.A. (music), 1935. Pp. viii, 374.
    Music and words of about 100 songs, with notes on the singers and circumstances of collection. Collected by the author through contacts made with his students at Southern State Normal University, 1932 and after.

493. Mackenzie, Mabel Laura Hunter. *The Scottish Ballad in the Eighteenth Century: A Bibliographical Study.* Toronto, Ph.D., 1955.

494. McKinley, Frank Arnold. *The American Gospel Song*. Westminster Choir Coll., M.A. (music), 1946.

495. McKissick, Marvin Leo. *A Study of the Function of Music in the Major Religious Revivals in America Since 1875*. So. California, M.M., 1957. Pp. 168, music.
    Reviews white revival music from 1875 to 1957; includes socioeconomic influences, the function of music in revival, and the evaluation of songs for possible use today.

496. McLean, Mervyn Evan. *Field Work in Maori Music: A Preliminary Study*. Otago, Honours M.A. (music), 1959. Pp. vi, 184, "Catalogue of Song Collections," glossary, map, music. *Pub.*: (in part) "A Preliminary Analysis of 87 Maori Chants," *Ethnomusicology* 8 (Jan. 1964), 41-48; "Oral Transmission in Maori Music," *Journal of the IFMC* 13 (1961), 59-62.
    Carried out in the Rotovua District of New Zealand between May and July of 1958.

497. McLean, Sammy Kay. *Aspects of the "Bänkelsang" in the Works of Bertolt Brecht*. Michigan, Ph.D. (lang. and lit.), 1963. Pp. 370. *D.A.* XXIV, 1618.
    Examines Brecht's work in its entirety as it relates to popular journalistic balladry in Germany. Musical instrumentation, the Brechtian actor as singer, form of his poems and songs, and the character and function of his music are among topics discussed.

498. McLeod, Norma. *The Social Context of Music in a Polynesian Community*. London (L.S.E.), M.A., 1956-57.

499. Macmillan, Cyrus J. *The Folk Songs of Canada*. Harvard, Ph.D., 1909. 2 vols. Pp. 1101, bibliog.
    Texts of 170 Canadian folksongs, often with several variations, with comments regarding origins of most of the songs.

500. MacOdrum, Murdock Maxwell. *Survival of the English and Scottish Popular Ballads in Nova Scotia: A Study of Folk-Song in Canada*. McGill U., M.A., 1924.

501. McPheeters, Dean William. *A Comparative Study of Some Spanish Songs and Ballads Collected in Tampa, Florida*. Florida, M.A., 1941. Pp. 118.

502. Madrid, Miguel Angel. *The Attitudes of the Spanish American People as Expressed in Their Coplas or Folk Songs.* Columbia U., Ph.D. (lang. and lit.), 1953. Pp. 139. *D.A.* XIV, 128.

Includes more than 3,000 *coplas*, representing the various Spanish American countries, gathered from existing printed collections.

503. Mahmoud, Parviz. *A Theory of Persian Music and Its Relation to Western Practice.* Indiana U., Ph.D. (music), 1956. Pp. iv, 164, bibliog., 123 musical exs. *D.A.* XVII, 1091.

A theory of Persian music, based on an analysis of twenty folk tunes and twelve *dastaghs*. Much consideration is given to tuning.

504. Mahr, Otto. *Das Volkslied im bäuerlichen Jahr der Rhön.* Frankfurt a.M. (phil.), 1938 (1939). *Pub.:* Frankfurt a.M., Diesterweg, 1939. Pp. 134.

505. Majumdar, Ambikacharan. *Die nordindische Musik der Gegenwart, unter Berücksichtigung der alten Theoretiker.* Königsberg (phil.), 1941. Pp. 16, 392, xiii.

506. Malm, William Paul. *Japanese Nagauta Music.* California (Los Angeles), Ph.D. (music), 1959. Vol. I: pp. 372, text; Vol. II: pp. 103, transcriptions. Awarded first prize in the Humanities among the Academy Monograph Prizes for 1959 offered by the American Academy of Arts and Sciences. *Pub.: Nagauta: The Heart of Kabuki Music* (Rutland, Vt. and Tokyo, Japan, Tuttle, 1963). Pp. 200, bibliog., illus., 100 pp. music insert.

507. Mann, Isak. *Zur Geschichte der synagogalen Musik.* Vienna (phil.), 1931.

508. Mansfield, Portia. *The Conchero Dancers of Mexico.* New York U., Ed.D. (anthro.), 1953. Pp. 319. *D.A.* XIII, 625.

Consists of an inquiry into: the prehispanic cultural background and the present-day culture, organizations and ritual; an analysis of three dances, with musical accompaniments and description of costumes and properties; a sound film, in color, of the Concheros, showing their cultural patterns, rituals, prayers, hymns, dances; a manual interpreting and supplementing the films.

509. Mares, Pablo. *Spanish-American Folk Songs and Dances of New Mexico.* Colorado S.C. of Ed., M.A. (music), 1946. Pp. 69.

510. Mark, Lindy Li. *The Structure of Inland Tlingit Music*. Northwestern U., M.A. (anthro.), 1955. Pp. 133, ii, bibliog., 70 music exs., scales, tables.

> Technical music analysis of songs recorded in the field in 1949-1951, not by the author. Includes material on song types, method, formal analysis, tonal analysis, melodic contour and rhythm, and description of songs.

511. Marquis, Robert Lincoln. *The Social Psychology of Music*. New York U., Ed.D., 1941. Pp. 261.

512. Marr, Marion E. *A Study of the Traditional Folk Festivals in Iowa: Their Contribution to the School Music Program*. So. California, M.M., 1952. Pp. 239, illus., music.

> Discusses survivals of European festivals in Iowa, and includes an appendix of music used.

513. Marsh, Lillian. *Latin American Music*. Northwestern U., M.M., 1943.

514. Marti, Anna Miller. *A History of the Ghost-Dance Religion Among the Indians*. Oklahoma, M.A. (hist.), 1935. Pp. 94, v.

> Taken largely from government documents, the author presents the history of a movement which began in 1889 with the appearance of a Paiute prophet, "who introduced certain dances and ceremonies which would hasten the destruction of the whites and the return of Indian civilization."

515. Martin, Raymond Jones. *The Transition from Psalmody to Hymnody in Southern Presbyterianism, 1753-1901*. Union Theol. Sem., D.S.M., 1963. Pp. 173. *D.A.* XXIV, 2512.

> Shows development from a period in which there existed a restriction to metrical versions of the Psalms, to a period in which a large proportion of hymns was set to a wide variety of tunes ranging from *Old Hundredth* to Victorian hymn tunes and American gospel melodies.

516. Maruyama, Y. *The Raga of India*. Tokyo U. Arts, 1959.

517. Mason, Charles Peter. *Personality Adjustment, Mental Maturity, and Music Aptitude of the Three Ethnic Groups Represented at Mt. Edgecumbe School, Mt. Edgecumbe, Alaska*. Central Wash. Coll. of Ed., M.Ed., 1955. Pp. 73, 15 tables.

> Tests used include the California Test of Mental Maturity, California Test of Personality, and Kwalwasser Music Talent Test. Conclusions: "Although there were some differences in the results of the personality test, the other tests failed to produce any indication of differences in mental maturity or music talent."

518. Mason, Gregory. *Culture of the Taironas.* So. California, Ph.D. (anthro.), 1938. Pp. 213, illus.

> Includes photographs of musical instruments and dances with some description of the latter. Primarily archaeological, based on original field research.

519. Materne, Gerd. *Die sozialen und wirtschaftlichen Probleme des Musikers.* Mannheim, 1953. Pp. 152.

520. Mathewson, Dorothy Ruth. *French-Canadian Folk-Songs.* McGill U., M.A., 1924.

521. Matsuo, F. *A Historical Study of the Lute, from the Ancient Orient to Mediaeval Europe.* Tokyo U. Arts, 1959.

522. Maxson, William L. *A Study of Modality and Folk Song in the Choral Music of Ralph Vaughan Williams.* Indiana U., M.M., 1957. Pp. iv, 77, bibliog., music.

> Analysis from the standpoint of meter, rhythm and tempo, melody, harmony, tonality, texture and formal structure.

523. May, Elizabeth. *Japanese Children's Music Before and After Contact with the West.* California (Los Angeles), Ph.D. (music), 1958. Pp. 205, bibliog., music, pls. *Pub.*: under the title *The Influence of the Meiji Period on Japanese Children's Music. Univ. of Calif. Pubs. in Music* 6 (Berkeley and Los Angeles, the Univ. of Calif. Press, 1963). Pp. xii, 95.

> Child-made songs and songs to be sung by children are discussed both before 1868, the beginning of the Meiji period, and after, when they were affected by the Western military band, Christian missionaries and Luther Whitney Mason, who worked with Japanese educators and musicians.

524. Mayer-Rosa, Norbert. *Studien zum deutschen Tagelied. Untersuchungen zur Gruppe "Tagelieder" in Uhlands Sammlung, "Alte hoch- und niederdeutsche Volkslieder."* Tübingen (phil.), 1938. Pp. 159.

> Johann Ludwig Uhland was the chief literary personality of a group of writers centered in Swabia early in the nineteenth century. His chief work on German folksong (1844) stands as a literal reproduction of the popular tradition of this genre.

525. Mayle, Bessie H. *History and Interpretation of the Pre-Reformation Carol and the Negro Spiritual.* Boston U., M.A. (music), 1932. Pp. 82, tables.

526. Mayne, Mabel DeLillian. *A Parallel Study of Ancient and Classical Greek Dance and Music.* Geo. Peabody, M.A. (phy. ed.), 1938. Pp. 121.

527. Mei, Ginsiang. *The Influence of Music on Chinese Culture.* Wayne State U., M.A. (music), 1952. Pp. 77.

> The role of music in Chinese high civilization, emphasizing Chinese drama, based on published sources by Chinese, European and American authors.

528. Mendelsohn, Ignaz. *Zur Entwicklung des deutschen Gesellschaftstanzes von 1750 bis 1850.* Vienna (phil.), 1925. Summary in *Studien zur Musikwiss.* 13 (1926).

529. Mercer, Hallie Nell. *Folk Tunes and Songs and Peoples that Make Them.* East Texas S.T.C., M.S. (music), 1943. Pp. 140.

530. Merriam, Alan P. *Instruments and Instrumental Usages in the History of Jazz.* Northwestern U., M.M., 1948. Pp. vi, 240, bibliog.

> Part I deals with a general history of jazz, but from the standpoint of developing instrumental techniques. Part II takes up each instrument in turn, and discusses its uses in the various periods of jazz, changes in its construction, technique, and so forth.

531. Merriam, Alan P. *Songs of the Afro-Bahian Cults: An Ethnomusicological Analysis.* Northwestern U., Ph.D. (anthro.), 1951. Pp. x, 464, bibliog., 64 charts and graphs, transcriptions of 98 songs, analysis of modal structures, appendixes.

> Technical analysis of songs of seven Bahian cult groups. Includes chapters on the Negro in Brazil, method of musical analysis, summary and conclusions which compare the music of the cults with each other, with West African, and with other New World Negro music.

532. Merrifield, Norman L. *A Comparison of Racial Differences as Shown by Musical Aptitude Tests.* Northwestern U., M.S. (educa.), 1932.

533. Merritt, Nancy G. *Negro Spirituals in American Collections; A Handbook for Students Studying Negro Spirituals.* Howard U., M.A. (engl.), 1940. Pp. 59, 44.

534. Mersmann, Hans. *Grundlagen einer musikal. Volksliedforschung.* Berlin, T.H. (HabSchr.), 1923. *Pub.: AfMw* 4-6 (1922-1924); and separately (Leipzig, Kistner & Siegel, 1930). Pp. 140.

535. Mertens, Käthe. *Die Entwicklung der englischen und schottischen Volksballaden im Verhältnis zu den dänischen Folkeviser.* Halle (phil.), 1920. Pp. 244.

536. Metzler, Fritz. *Tonalität und melodische Struktur der älteren deutschen und nordischen Volksweise mit besonderer Berücksichtigung der isländischen Kleinmelodik.* Tübingen (phil.), 1950. Pp. v, 192.

537. Meyer, Henry E. *Southern Spirituals from White Singers.* Southwestern U., M.A., 1942.

538. Meyer, Leonard B. *Emotion and Meaning in Music.* Chicago, Ph.D. (hist. of culture), 1954. Pp. 473. *Pub.:* Chicago, Univ. of Chicago Press, 1956. Pp. 307, illus.

539. Midland, Emil Querineau. *Portuguese Folk Music in Santa Clara County, California.* Stanford U., M.A. (educa.), 1946. Pp. 53.

540. Millar, Branford P. *British Balladry in the Eighteenth Century.* Harvard, Ph.D., 1946. Pp. 461, bibliog.
    Includes edition of the Dicey Catalogue of Old Ballads (Bodleian) with additions and notes made by Bishop Percy. Annotated, with an index of first lines and bibliographies of ballad collections, catalogs and indexes.

541. Miller, Kurt Robert. *Heroes Found in Song Texts from Folk Music of the U. S.* So. California, D.M.A., 1963. 2 vols. Pp. 642. *D.A.* XXIV, 3782.
    Investigation consisted of a thorough examination of folksong texts to (1) identify heroes, (2) discover their character traits, (3) rate the degree of emphasis given to each trait in the same occupational group, (4) compile a list of the traits in order to identify the nature of a composite individual representing the folk hero of the U. S.

542. Miller, Louise. *Folk Music in Louisiana.* Northwestern U., M.M., 1940. Pp. 52, bibliog., music.
    Proposes to determine origin of Louisiana folk music. Contains a

review of similar studies, description of the effects on Louisiana folk music of the French, Spanish, British, American Indians, and Negroes, and influences from other states.

543. Mitzelfelt, Harold Ezra. *The Nationalistic Trend in Contemporary Mexican Music.* Washington, M.A. (music), 1945. Pp. 138, bibliog.

Historical survey of influence on contemporary Mexican music. Discusses Maya, Aztec, present-day Indians, and influence of European colonization. Musical examples demonstrate the folk idioms present in modern compositions.

544. Moffatt, Ruth Jennings. *The Dance in the Life of the Early Greeks.* Geo. Peabody, M.A. (phy. ed.), 1932. Pp. 62.

545. Mohling, Virginia Gill. *Twana Spirit Power Songs.* Washington, M.A. (anthro.), 1957. Pp. 40, bibliog., 29 transcriptions.

(1) Ethnographic setting of spirit power songs in Twana (Northwest Coast, Puget Sound) culture; (2) analysis of mode, tonality, intervals, range, form, contour, rhythm, and correlation of text with melody; (3) song transcriptions with ethnographic annotations, and text translations.

546. Montague, J. Harold. *A Historical Survey of Negro Music and Musicians and Their Influence on Twentieth Century Music.* Syracuse U., M.A. (music), 1929. Pp. 52, bibliog., music.

Includes chapters on African music, Negro folksongs in the United States, Negro musicians of the Old World and in America, twentieth century Negro music and musicians, and the influence of Negro music and musicians on twentieth century composers.

547. Montgomery, Guy. *Some Representative Songs of the Lower Races, Edited and Annotated, with an Essay on the Cultural Background of These Races.* California (Berkeley), M.A. (engl.), 1917. Pp. 198, music, tables.

The bulk of the thesis consists of song texts drawn from early explorers' accounts. The aim is to trace "literary change, or evolution, which is closely related to change in habits, customs, and beliefs . . . ." Theoretical material is drawn from Morgan and Ratzel; there is no discussion of musical aspects.

548. Montgomery, Guy. *Studies in Primitive Folksong.* California (Berkeley), Ph.D. (engl.), 1920. Pp. 124, bibliog., music. *Pub.*: (in part) under the title "A Method of Studying the Structure of Primitive Verse Applied to the Songs of the Teton Sioux," Univ. of Calif., *Pubs. in Modern Philol.* 11 (1922), pp. 269-83.

Considers the literary aspects of primitive folksong, devoting no space to music *per se*. The primary concern of the author is to fit song texts into an evolutionary scheme, using the theoretical position of L. H. Morgan.

549. Montgomery, Margaret Lucile. *A Study of the American Versions of "Barbara Allen."* Indiana U., M.A., 1935. Pp. ii, 106, "Bibliography of Versions . . . ," tables.
> The thesis applies the historic-geographic method to reconstruct the archetype from which variants have grown, to show the regional dissemination, and to indicate the changes which have taken place. Using this method, the author attempted to determine if the versions in the U.S. contain motifs that are original and distinct from those in the English and Scottish versions, and, if so, if it was evident from this that a second period of the creating of the ballads of the Child type has been inaugurated in the New World. The conclusions were negative.

550. Morgan, Wesley K. *The Development of the Wesleyan Hymnody.* Union Theol. Sem., M.A. (music), 1946.

551. Morgues, Marcelle. *La Danse provençale.* Aix, thèse lettres, 1955. *Pub.*: Cannes, Robaudy, 1956. Pp. 164, music, pls., port.

552. Morik, Werner. *Johannes Brahms und sein Verhältnis zum deutschen Volkslied.* Göttingen (phil.), 1953. Pp. 301.

553. Morris, Alton Chester. *Folk Songs of Florida and Their Cultural Background.* North Carolina, Ph.D. (engl. lit.), 1941.

554. Morris, Arthur Corwin, Jr. *Music in Rhode Island, 1630-1820.* Brown U., M.A. (music), 1960. Pp. 78, bibliog.
> Deals with Puritanism and early music in Colonial America.

555. Morris, Robert Othello. *The Folk Music of California for the Period 1769 to 1860 Available for Use in the Secondary Social Studies.* So. California, M.M., 1948. Pp. 163, music.
> Lists available music from that era and discusses its possible use in the schools.

556. Morris, Ruth Dean. *An Analysis of Mexican Folk Music.* Eastman, M.M. (music theory), 1949. Pp. iv, 67, illus., music.
> The author, having lived the greater part of her life near the Mexican border, believes that the folk melodies will have a decided influence on the development of Mexican national music. Some analysis.

557. Morton, David. *Modal Practice in Traditional Thai Music.* California (Los Angeles), Ph.D. In process.

558. Morton, Jean. *Some Physiological Effects of Jazz and Classical Music.* Pittsburgh, M.A. (psychol.), 1935. Pp. 29, tables.
"The study raises questions rather than answering them."

559. Morton, Maralyn Bertha. *Studies in Oral Verse in the United States.* Chicago, A.M. (engl.), 1921. Pp. 108, xiv, bibliog.
The study is concerned, mainly from a literary standpoint, with types of indigenous song that reflect phases of life in the United States. Categories discussed include Negro folksongs, frontier and adventure songs, songs of outlaws and criminals, miscellaneous songs (river, railroad, war, sailor). Some texts, no music.

560. Moser, Hans Joachim. *Die Musikergenossenschaften im deutschen Mittelalter.* Rostock (phil.), 1910. Pp. viii, 130.

561. Moyle, Alice. *The Intervalic Structure of Australian Aboriginal Singing.* Sydney, M.A., Honours (music), 1957. Pp. 140, map, 72 music transcriptions, 55 "interval charts" or skeletal transcriptions.
A general survey of musical characteristics based on recorded material available at the time. Deals with intervallic "situations," aurally assessed, not frequency measurements.

562. Müller, Auguste. *Das plattdeutsche Kinderlied. Eine metrische Studie.* Kiel (phil.), 1915. Pp. 209.

563. Müller, Max. *Jean-Joseph Vadé (1719-1757) und das Vaudeville.* Greifswald (phil.), 1911. Pp. xviii, 174.

564. Müller, Wilhelm. *Über die Musik der muslimischen Voelker (Araber).* Erlangen (phil.), 1922. Pp. vii, 38.

565. Muir, Donald. *The Song that Stings; An Analysis of Political Satire in American Musical Theatre, 1929-1941.* Stanford U., Ph.D., 1963.

566. Munro, Kathleen. *The Role of Music in the Development of Educational Thought Among the Early Classical Greeks.* Washington, Ph.D., 1937. Pp. 189.

567. Murray, Eloise. *Contribution of the American Indian to Leisure Time.* Geo. Peabody, M.A., 1934. Pp. 168, illus.
General consideration of games, dances, arts, crafts.

568. Nagahiro, H. *Theory of Indian Music and Its Philosophical Background.* Tokyo U. Arts, 1961.

569. Nagatsugawa, T. *Musical Instruments on the Reliefs of Borobudur.* Tokyo U. Arts, 1957.

570. Nandris, Octavian. *La Chanson populaire roumaine et sa stylistique.* Paris, thèse complémentaire lettres, 1948.

571. Nash, Dennison J. *The American Composer: A Study in Social-Psychology.* Pennsylvania, Ph.D. (sociol.), 1954. Pp. 254. *D.A.* XIV, 879.
Role, life history, personality, attitude and behavior of twenty-three American-born composers of art music were studied.

572. Neal, Mabel Evangeline. *Brown County Songs and Ballads Collected and Annotated by M. E. Neal.* Indiana U., A.M., 1926. Pp. 14, 183, bibliog., music.
100 songs, about one third including unharmonized melodies, given "as they were sung by the older people of Brown County, Indiana 20 to 40 years ago." Comparative notes discuss music and words, and give references to sources and distribution for each song.

573. Nelson, Carl Leonard. *The Sacred and Secular Music of the Swedish Settlers of the Midwest, 1841-1917.* New York U., Ph.D. (music ed.), 1950. Pp. 167. *D.A.* XI, 130.
Examines music performed and composed in the religious, educational and home and community background.

574. Nettl, Bruno. *Musical Culture of the Arapaho.* Indiana U., A.M. (music), 1951. Pp. vi, 116, bibliog., 4 tables, 3 illus., 42 transcriptions.
Deals with the ethnology, instruments, styles, and texts of Arapaho music.

575. Nettl, Bruno. *American Indian Music North of Mexico: Its Styles and Areas.* Indiana U., Ph.D. (music), 1953. Pp. vii, 239, bibliog., 8 maps (2 folding), 6 tables, 11 music exs., 22 transcriptions. *D.A.* XIII, 834. *Pub.: North American Indian Musical Styles.* Amer. Folklore Soc., *Memoirs* 45 (Phila., 1954). Pp. ix, 51, map, music.
General characteristics; division of North American Indian music into seven areas and fourteen styles; comparison of musical areas with cultural and linguistic areas.

576. Neumann, Rudi. *Das deutsche Volkslied im Weltkriege.* Greifswald (phil.), 1921. Pp. 126.

577. Newberry, Josephine. *Legends and Festivals Associated with
Indigenous Dances of Mexico.* Texas, M.A. (phy. ed.), 1942.
Pp. 98.

578. Newey, Donald Wesley. *A Study of Some Assyrian Folk Songs
Performed in the United States.* Northwestern U., M.M., 1957.
Pp. 85, 9 music exs.
> Based on original research. Gives transcription and analysis of
> nine Assyrian songs recorded in Chicago, plus chapters on mu-
> sical instruments, and summary.

579. Nickerson, Camille L. *Africo-Creole Music in Louisiana; A
Thesis on the Plantation Songs Created by the Creole Negroes
of Louisiana.* Oberlin C., M.A., 1932.

580. Nickel, Margaret Elizabeth. *American Folk-Music.* Northwestern U., M.M., 1942. Pp. 69, bibliog. (189 titles).
> A study to determine whether the United States has a represen-
> tative folk music. Discusses music of early settlers, Indians,
> Negroes, cowboys; the fusion of foreign elements; and possibil-
> ities for the future.

581. Nikolov, Kosta. *Beiträge zum Studium des bulgarischen Volksliedes. Metrik—Rhythmik—Tonalität.* Berlin (phil.), 1942. Pp.
106.

582. Obreschkoff, Christo. *Das bulgarische Volkslied.* Bern (phil.),
1937. *Pub.: Berner Veröff. zur Musikforschung* 9 (Bern, Haupt,
1937). Pp. iv, 106.

583. O'Brien, Margaret Theresa. *The Influence of Irish Folk-Songs
and Folk-Lore on English Literature.* McGill U., M.A., 1928.

584. Oehler, Fritz. *Die Weise des neueren deutschen Volksliedes.*
Marburg (phil.), 1943. *Pub.: Musik und Schrifttum* 3 (Würzburg, Triltsch, 1943). Pp. 174.

585. O'Hara, Ruth. *A Study of the Dances of Early California.* So.
California, M.S. (educa.), 1938. Pp. 139.

586. Oka, H. *A Study of Tala in Karnatic Music.* Tokyo U. Arts,
1960.

587. O'Neill, P. G. *Sarugaku, Dengaku and Kusemai in the Creation of Nō Drama, 1300-1450.* London, Ph.D., 1957.

588. Onion, Charles Clary. *The Social Status of Musicians in Seventeenth Century France.* Minnesota, Ph.D. (hist.), 1959. Pp. 208, bibliog., tables. *D.A.* XX, 2238.

> After an introduction which considers patronage, national traits and prejudices, other contemporary art forms and the influence of institutions, opera and political events that affected music, the author devotes chapters to the musician in regard to "La Maison"; "Wages, Income and Property"; "Dowries and Marriage"; and ". . . the Social Ladder."

589. Ordelheide, Nancy. *Transcription of Polyphonic Music, 900-1600, with an Electronic Digital Computer.* Washington U., Ph.D. In process.

590. Ornstein, Ruby. *Balinese Gamelan Anklung.* California (Los Angeles), Ph.D. In process.

591. Owens, William A. *Texas Folk Songs.* Iowa, Ph.D. (engl.), 1941. Pp. v, 231.

> 120 songs transcribed from 500 separate items recorded by the author in Louisiana, Oklahoma, Missouri and Texas over the previous ten years. Classified as British and American Traditional Ballads and Songs; Children's Songs and Games; Cowboy Songs; Negro Spirituals; Play-Party Songs; Miscellaneous Songs.

592. Ozley, Clara Elizabeth. *Christmas Customs and Carols from Latin America.* Northwestern U., M.M., 1945.

593. Palecziska, Herbert. *Die Entwicklung der altösterreichischen Militärmusikkapellen.* Vienna (phil.), 1939. Pp. 176.

594. Palikarova Verdeil, Raina. *La Musique byzantine chez les bulgares et les russes du Xe au XIVe siècle.* Paris, thèse lettres, 1948. *Pub.: Monumenta Musicae Byzantinae* 8 (Copenhagen, 1953). Pp. 249.

595. Palmquist, Marjorie J. *Twelve Mexican Folk Songs Selected and Arranged for High School Mixed Chorus.* Iowa, M.A. (music), 1940.

596. Panke, Fritz. *Die schottischen Liebesballaden. Ein Beitrag zur Entstehung von Variantbildungen.* Marburg (phil.), 1935. *Pub.: Neue deutsche Forschungen. Abt. Engl. Philologie* 4 (Bd. 53 d. Gesamtreihe), (Berlin, Junker & Dünnhaupt, 1935). Pp. 131.

597. Parcels, D. B. *The Importance of Folk Song in the Development of World Citizenship.* So. California, M.M., 1943. Pp. 110, music.
> Shows similar functions of folk music in the world, as well as its special character in specific countries.

598. Parke, Fandee Young (Mrs.). *A Study of the Musical Talents of the Negro, Mexican and White Children in the Public Schools of San Marcos, Texas.* Southwest Texas S.T.C., M.A., 1938. Pp. 60.

599. Parker, Olin Griffith. *A Study of the Relationship of Aesthetic Sensitivity to Musical Ability, Intelligence, and Socioeconomic Status.* Kansas, Ed.D. (music), 1961. Pp. 168. *D.A.* XXII, 2416.
> Subjects were 1174 Kansas high school students. The relationship to musical ability was moderate, to intelligence, slight, and to socioeconomic status, negligible.

600. Parks, Edna Dorintha. *English Hymns and Their Tunes in the Sixteenth and Seventeenth Centuries.* Boston U., Ph.D. (music), 1957. Pp. 455. *D.A.* XVII, 1778.
> Examination of 1027 pre-Isaac Watts hymn tunes.

601. Parr, Annie Ruth. *A Study of European Folk Songs Collected in Waukegan, Illinois.* Northwestern U., M.M., 1951. Pp. ii, 66, bibliog., 30 music exs., scale patterns.
> Based on original research. After a general introduction and chapter on method, gives melodies and texts of Finnish, Swedish, Slovenian, Armenian and Jewish folksongs. Summary chapter contains brief analysis.

602. Patterson, Cecil Lloyd. *A Different Drum; the Image of the Negro in the Nineteenth Century Popular Song Books.* Pennsylvania, Ph.D. (lang. and lit.), 1961. Pp. 268. *D.A.* XXII, 1161.
> The sample consisted of approximately 260 songbooks and 96 writings representing both "popular" and "elite" literature of all the forms except the essay. Most references to the Negro were in the middle decades and pictured the Negro as endowed with exceptional musical ability, a distinctive sense of humor, a carefree disposition and a great capacity for loyalty.

603. Patterson, John S. *The Folksong Revival and Some Sources of the Popular Image of the Folksinger: 1920-1963.* Indiana U., M.A. (folkl.), 1963. Pp. ii, 97, bibliog.

Attempts to bring together material pertinent to the revival and to outline its history, paying particular attention to the revival's appeal to various groups and its relationship to mass media.

604. Patton, Marian. *Music in Negro Schools of the College Level.* Eastman, M.M., 1940.

605. Paulsen, George W. *A History of Scandinavian Music Up to the Year 1800.* New York U., M.A. (music), 1942. Pp. 151.

606. Pauntscheff, Stoyan. *Über den epischen Gesang in Bulgarien.* Prague (phil.), 1934.

607. Pawlowska, Harriet. *Polish Folk Songs Gathered in Detroit, with an Analysis of the Music by Grace L. Engel.* Wayne State U., M.A., *ca.* 1940. Pp. 57, 41 songs with music and texts in Polish.

A good collection of European material in an American urban tradition. Transcriptions are moderately reliable, analysis uses rather obsolete methods. Brief introduction on the cultural background of the informants is included. Exists only on microfilm.

608. Payne, E. M. *The Folk-Song Element in the Music of Vaughan Williams.* Liverpool, Ph.D., 1952-53.

609. Peach, Everett. *The Gospel Song; Its Influences on Christian Hymnody.* Wayne State U., M.A. (music), 1960. Pp. 113, bibliog., music.

Includes references to gospel music in oral tradition.

610. Penner, Eva Nelly. *Public School Music in El Salvador.* North Dakota, Ph.D. (educa.), 1946. Pp. 136.

611. Pernecky, John Martin. *The Historical and Musico-Ethnological Approach to the Instrumental Compositions of Béla Bartók.* Northwestern U., Ph.D. (music), 1956. Pp. viii, 184, bibliog., music. *D.A.* XVI, 2476.

Attempts to trace the influence and development of the peasant songs which Bartók collected in the Balkan and Asiatic areas and which then became part of his own compositional writing. Chapters on Bartók as ethnologist, ethnic characterictics in Bartók's melody and in his rhythm, and ethnic horizontal and vertical intervallic relationships in his music.

612. Petermann, Kurt. *Das Quodlibet—eine Volksliedquelle?* Leipzig (phil.), 1960 (1961). 2 vols.

613. Pfeiffer, William R. *A Musical Analysis of Some Ritual Songs of the Manobo of North Central Cotabato on Mindanao Island in the Philippines.* Hawaii, M.A. (music), 1965. Pp. vii, 215, music.

   A transcription and musical analysis of 11 ritual songs from the field recordings collected by Priscilla Magdamo Abraham.

614. Philips, Mary K. *A Study of the Sources of Welsh Music in America and an Analysis and Evaluation of the Welsh-American Contribution to the Folk and Art Music of This Country.* Claremont C., M.A., 1948. Pp. 166, figs., music, tables.

   "It is the writer's intention to show (1) that the Welsh folk element and interest in music as a whole is widespread in this country; (2) that it is very much alive; (3) that it is not confined to a 'peasant' element as so much of folk music is; (4) and that it is a fund of excellent musical material in form and content which should be utilized in the building of a native American music and interest therein."

615. Pian, Rulan Chao (Mrs.). *Sources of Music in the Sung Dynasty: 960-1279 A.D.* Radcliffe C., Ph.D. (music), 1960. Pp. 306.

616. Pierson, Lolita B. *Greek Music in Its Social Aspects.* Oregon, M.A. (music), 1943. Pp. 202.

617. Platel, Marguerite. *Vom Volkslied zum Gesellschaftslied. Zur Geschichte des Liedes im 16. und 17. Jahrhundert.* Bern (phil.), 1938. *Pub.: Sprache u. Dichtung* 64 (Bern, Haupt, 1939). Pp. xv, 133.

618. Pöhlmann, Egert. *Griechische Musikfragmente. Ein Weg zur altgriechischen Musik.* Erlangen (phil.), 1960. *Pub.: Erlanger Beitr. zur Sprach- und Kunstwiss.* 8 (Nuremberg, Carl, 1960). Pp. vi, 84.

619. Pohl, Gerhard. *Der Strophenbau im deutschen Volkslied.* Berlin (phil.), 1920. Pp. viii, 74. *Pub.: Palaestra* 136 (Berlin, Mayer & Müller, 1921). Pp. viii, 219.

620. Poladian, Sirvart V. *Folk Songs of Asia Minor.* California (Berkeley), M.A. (music), 1938. Pp. 75 text, 4 pp. bibliog., 12 pp. of common tonal patterns.

Analysis of 253 Armenian folksongs collected about 1900 by Komitas Keworkian. Descriptions of intervals, ranges and contours, tonality, rhythm and meter, and tonal form.

621. Polter, Karl-Heinz. *Musik als Heilmittel.* Münster (with Med. Akad. Düsseldorf) (med.), 1934. Pp. iv, 59.

622. Pommer, Mechthild. *Dr. Josef Pommer und das deutsche Volkslied.* Prague (phil.), 1941. Pp. 206.

623. Popowa, Liljana. *Studien zur Tonalität und Melodik des bulgarischen Volksliedes aus Ost- und Westthrazien.* Frankfurt a.M. (phil.), 1948. Pp. vii, 200.

624. Pouinard, Alfred. *Recherches sur la musique d'origine française en Amerique du Nord: Canada et Louisiane.* Laval U., Ph.D. (music), 1951.

625. Powers, Harold Stone. *The Background of the South Indian Raga-System.* Princeton U., Ph.D. (music), 1959. Vol. I: pp. xv, 222, text and bibliography; Vol. II: pp. 84, iii, text; pp. 10, music exs. *D.A.* XXI, 206.

> Vol. I is divided into two parts: The Synthesis of Theory and Practice; Analysis of Svaras and Phrases.

626. Prudhommeau, Germaine. *La Danse grecque antique.* Paris, thèse lettres, 1955. Pp. 228.

627. Pugh, Grace Thompson. *Historical Background and Significance of Mexican Folk Dances.* Southwest Texas S.T.C., M.A., 1945. Pp. 49.

628. Purdy, William Earl. *Music in Mormon Culture, 1830-1876.* Northwestern U., Ph.D. (music), 1960. Pp. 384. *D.A.* XXI, 3116.

> Music in education and the theater; military and community bands; and folksongs, hymns and religious songs are discussed.

629. Putnam, Maxine Schannep. *The Extent to Which the Folk-Song Appears in the Music Study of Elementary Schools.* Florida State, M.A. (educa.), 1931.

630. Pyke, Launcelot Allen, II. *George Gershwin; A Study of His Style.* Michigan, M.A. (music), 1946. Pp. 59.

631. Pyke, Launcelot Allen, II. *Jazz, 1920 to 1927: An Analytical Study.* Iowa, Ph.D. (music), 1963. 2 vols.: pp. iv, 115; iv, 82, bibliog., diagrs., music. *D.A.* XXIII, 2937.

> Vol. I contains an analysis of the music characteristics of jazz at the high point of its New Orleans ensemble period as found in the recorded versions of ten jazz tunes performed in the 1920's. Vol. 2 consists of the scores of the ten tunes analyzed, as transcribed from the recordings.

632. Quasten, Johannes. *Musik und Gesang in den heidnischen Kulten der Antike und im Christentum der ersten Jahrhunderte.* Münster (theol.), 1928. Pp. 52. *Pub.: Liturgiegeschichtliche Quellen und Forschungen* 25 (Münster, Aschendorff, 1930). Pp. xii, 274.

633. Quintana, Bertha Beatrice. *The Deep Song of the Andalusian Gypsies: A Study of the Transmission and Perpetuation of Traditional Culture Themes.* New York U., Ed.D. (anthro.), 1960. Pp. 282. *D.A.* XXI, 1020.

> Origins and perpetuation of Deep Song were studied, and its form, meaning, use and function identified. Data obtained from literary sources and field work.

634. Radin, Paul. *The Ritual and Significance of the Winnebago Medicine Dance.* Columbia U., Ph.D. (anthro.), 1911. Pp. ii, 159, bibliog., vita. *Pub.: J. of Amer. Folklore* 24 (1911), pp. 149-208.

> Describes Winnebago ritual, organization of bands, division of ceremony and component elements, types of speeches, songs and action, the Ojibwa Midewiwin and Menominee type, significance of ritual complexes, summary.

635. Rainbow, Edward L. *A Pilot Study to Investigate Constructs of Musical Aptitude.* Iowa, Ph.D. (music), 1963. Pp. 194. *D.A.* XXIV, 770.

> The purpose of the study was to give the constructors of future musical aptitude tests objective direction for the establishment of construct validity. 14 variables were used in the empirical investigation.

636. Rankin, Dorothy. *Music and Musical Instruments in Classical Rome.* Oklahoma, M.A. (classical langs. and lit.), 1939. Pp. 79, iii.

> Data from a study of the private and public activities in which music had a part.

637. Rearick, Elizabeth Charlotte. *Dances of the Hungarians: A Study of the Dances Found Today in Hungary, Together with a Description of Some of the Peasant Festivities.* Columbia T.C., Ph.D., 1939. *Pub.:* Columbia Univ. *Contribs. to Educa.,* No. 770. Pp. viii, 151, bibliog., choreog., figs., map, music.
Deals with the social significance of Hungarian folk dances, their origin and original purpose in folklore.

638. Rebling, Eberhard. *Die soziologischen Grundlagen der Stilwandlung der Musik in Deutschland um die Mitte des 18. Jahrhunderts.* Berlin (phil.), 1935. Pp. 135.

639. Reece, Cortez Donald. *A Study of Selected Folksongs Collected Mainly in Southern West Virginia.* So. California, Ph.D. (music), 1955. 2 vols. Pp. 1049, map, music.
Presentation of material gathered by the author in the field with special attention to classification, variants, and notation.

640. Regier, Ruth. *A Survey of Patronage in the Development of the Professional Musician.* Kansas, M.A. (music), 1939. Pp. 79.

641. Regner, Hermann. *Taktwechselnde Volkstänze im Schwäbischen Ries.* Munich (phil.), 1957. Pp. 149, illus., map, music.

642. Reich, Othmar. *Das Qualitätsproblem. Eine musikpsychologisch-psychologische Abhandlung.* Prague (phil.), 1932.

643. Reimer, Arthur Louis. *Mexican Indian Folk Music and Its Educational Values.* So. California, M.S. (educa.), 1947.
Aztec, Zapotec, Huichol, Tarascan, Otomí, Mazatec.

644. Reinhard, Kurt. *Die Musik Birmas.* Munich (phil.), 1938 (1939). *Pub.: Schriftenreihe des Musikwiss. Seminars der Universität München* 5 (Würzburg, Triltsch, 1939). Pp. 106, 41.

645. Reinhard, Kurt. *Musikinstrumente und Musikkulturkreise. Versuch einer primär musikwissenschaftlichen Instrumentenkunde.* Berlin, F.U. (HabSchr.), 1950. Pp. iii, 170, table. An abstract of the supplement, under the title "Beitrag zu einer neuen Systematik der Musikinstrumente," appears in *Die Musikforschung* 13 (1960), pp. 160-164.

646. Reschke, Johannes. *Studie zur Geschichte der brandenburgisch-preussischen Heeresmusik.* Berlin (phil.), 1936. Pp. 96.

647. Reyes, Francisca S. *Philippine Folk Dances and Games.* Philippines, M.A., 1926.

648. Reynolds, Sarah Gertrude. *The Development and Evolution of the Dance.* Geo. Peabody, M.A. (phy. ed.), 1937. Pp. 41.

649. Richards, Zaneta Hooulu. *The Maori Action Song.* Hawaii, M.A. (pacific islands studies). In process.
    A study of social context and musical content.

650. Richter, Lukas. *Zur Wissenschaftslehre von der Musik bei Platon und Aristoteles.* Berlin, H.U. (phil.), 1957. Pp. 269. *Pub.:* "Die Aufgaben der Musiklehre nach Aristoxenos und Klaudios Ptolemäus." In: *AfMw* 15 (1958), pp. 209-229.

651. Ricks, George Robinson. *A Subjective Description of the Afro-Bahian Cults and Their Music.* Northwestern U., M.M., 1949. Pp. 62, bibliog., music, 9 pls.
    Includes chapters on the cults, their music, and the importance of understanding the African style. Appendix includes examples transcribed by Richard A. Waterman.

652. Ricks, George Robinson. *Some Aspects of the Religious Music of the United States Negro: An Ethnomusicological Study with Special Emphasis on the Gospel Tradition.* Northwestern U., Ph.D. (anthro.), 1960. Pp. 428, bibliog., music. *D.A.* XXI, 1020.
    An "investigation with a view toward throwing some light on the processes through which the United States Negro has retained African musical values and . . . has integrated musical elements from European culture . . . ." Representative music from three style periods—Spiritual (pre-Civil War), Jubilee (post-Civil War), and Gospel (1900 to date)—is analyzed.

653. Ridley, Harriette Gower. *Music in the Life of Man.* New York U., Ph.D., 1942.
    Discusses religious beliefs, social customs, and cultural achievements of man through the years as expressed in music.

654. Riebe, Charmetta. *UNESCO and Intercultural Music Education: Folk Music Teaching in Europe and in the United States under UNESCO Teacher-Exchange Basis.* Michigan, M.A., 1950.

655. Riedel, Herbert. *Die Darstellung von Musik und Musikerlebnis in der erzählenden deutschen Dichtung.* Bonn (phil.), 1956.

Pub.: under the title *Musik und Musikerlebnis* . . . . In *Abhandlungen zur Kunst-, Musik- und Literaturwissenschaft* 12 (Bonn, Bouvier, 1959). Pp. 702.

656. Riegler, Emil. *Studien über das rumänische Volkslied.* Vienna (phil.), 1927.

657. Riehl, William, Jr. *A Survey of Iberian Folk Song, Its Origins, Characteristics and Influence.* Catholic U., M.A. (music), 1944. Pp. 63, glossary, music.
   A discussion of the various influences, Arabian, Gypsy and Byzantine, which contributed to the Spanish "idiom" in music. Instances of the Spanish influence in the works of certain French and Russian composers are cited.

658. Rigel, Ruth Ann. *The Historical Development of American Folk Dances.* Iowa, M.A. (phy. ed.), 1942.

659. Riley, James. *Ethos in Greek Music.* Coll.-Conserv. of Music of Cincinnati, M.M., 1948. Pp. 89, bibliog.
   Discusses origins and theory of Greek music and ethos, source references for Greek music.

660. Rivais, Irene. *Fusion of the Arts in the Green Corn Dance of the Eastern Pueblos of New Mexico.* Wayne State U., M.A. (essay) (humanit.), 1961. Pp. 61, illus., music.
   Includes comments on Pueblo music in its relationship to visual arts and poetry, based on the published literature and on the author's field notes.

661. Robinson, K. G. *A Critical Study of Chu Tsai Yü's Account of the System of the Lü or Twelve Musical Tubes in Ancient China.* Oxford (U.C.), B. Litt., 1950-51.

662. Robinson, Mabel L. *American Negro Folk Music; the Evolution of Its Structure and Technique.* Boston U., M.A., 1940. Pp. [4] 99, bibliog., music.

663. Rogers, Fern. *Creative Music for African Children.* So. California, A.M. (music), 1946. Pp. 257, music.
   Based on teaching experience in Kavirondo, the thesis starts with African music and works into the Euro-American styles.

664. Rogers, *Sister* Mary James. *Elements of Musical Study in the Missionary School and in Some Missions Afar.* Catholic U., M.A., 1938. Pp. 99.
   Includes Maryknoll missions in China, Japan and Korea.

665. Rogers, Ruth Audrey. *French Canadian Folk Music.* Northwestern U., M.M., 1947. Pp. 115, bibliog., 52 music exs.

Discusses background of French Canadian folk music and gives examples with very brief analysis.

666. Roller, Gilbert Harvey. *The Development of the Methods for Analysis of Musical Compositions and for the Formation of a Symmetrical Twelve-tone Row Using the Electronic Digital Computer.* Michigan State U., Ph.D. (music ed.), 1964. Pp. 487. *D.A.* XXV, 2555.

Among other findings, the results of an analysis made were those showing the frequency of repetition of the melodic intervals in each voice, along with the frequency of intervals between successive roots, both with indications as to the upward and downward movements. A Control Data Company 160A computer was used, but all programs developed are adaptable to the large 3600 computer.

667. Romansky, Ljubomir. *Die einfachen Koledo-Refrains der bulgarischen Weihnachtslieder.* Berlin (phil.), 1940 (1942). *Pub.: Sbornik na Bulgarskata d Akademija na naukitě* 36, 4 (1942), pp. 297-614.

668. Rosch, Gisela. *Das deutsche Kiltlied. Eine Untersuchung über die Zusammenhänge zwischen Volkslied, Kunstlied und volkstümlichen Leben.* Tübingen (phil.), 1957. Pp. viii, 491, maps, tables.

669. Ross, Verne Ralph. *The Relations Between Intelligence, Scholastic Achievement, and Musical Talent of Three Racial Groups.* So. California, Ph.D. (music ed.), 1931. Pp. 285, bibliog., graphs, tables. *Pub.:* (in part) *Jour. of Juv. Res.* 20 (1936), pp. 47-64.

A comparison of scores on the Seashore test received by 427 Indian, 365 Japanese, and 1,541 white children, in grades 4 to 12, with related studies of correlations between musical ability, intelligence and various scholastic measures. The thesis in general confirms the findings of the maker of the test.

670. Rothe, Hans-Joachim. *Alte deutche Volkslieder und ihre Bearbeitungen durch Isaac, Senfl und Othmayr.* Leipzig (phil.), 1957. Pp. 293, music.

Heinrich Isaac (*ca.* 1450-1517), Ludwig Senfl (*ca.* 1490-*ca.* 1543) and Kasper Othmayr (1515-1553) were influenced by and utilized the folk music of the various countries in which they lived.

671. Rowntree, Mildred L. (Mrs.). *Cultural Potential of German Folk Music in Modern Teaching.* Sul Ross S.C., M.A., 1954.

672. Runge, Herbert. *Die Melodien ostpreussischer Volkslieder. Versuch zur Feststellung eines landschaftlich gebundenen Liedtypus.* Königsberg (phil.), 1939. Pp. 59.

673. Ruppenthal, Ethel E. *The Social Significance of Music.* Kansas, M.A. (music ed.), 1939.

674. Ruppert, Johann. *Der Volksliederschatz eines Spessartdorfes.* Würzburg (phil.), 1915. *Pub.: Blätter zur bayerischen Volkskunde* 4 (1915), pp. 1-60.

675. Sadler, Cora. *Creole Songs.* Michigan, M.A. (music), 1939. Pp. vi, 254, bibliog., music.
    Deals with types and varieties, form and musical details and influence of Creole songs.

676. Salmen, Walter. *Der fahrende Musiker im spätmittelalterlichen Europa.* Saarbrücken (HabSchr.), 1959. *Pub.: Die Musik im alten und neuen Europa* 4 (Kassel, Hinnenthal, 1960). Pp. 244.

677. Saltzman, Herbert Royce. *An Historical Study of the Function of Music Among the Brethren of Christ.* So. California, D.M.A., 1964. Pp. 346. *D.A.* XXV, 1957.
    Considers music as it relates to the devotional, social and educational programs of the church community.

678. Sami Hafez, Muhammed Mahmud. *La Connaissance de la musique égyptienne en France avant 1850.* Paris, thèse lettres, 1954. Pp. 327.

679. Saran, Anirudha Behari. *Ethnography of Tehri-Garhwal, a Himalayan District in India.* Indiana U., A.M. (anthro.), 1955. Pp. vi, 125.
    Pp. 52-53: musical instruments; pp. 97-99: folk dances and folksongs; a cultural, rather than a musical description of three songs and dances.

680. Saucier, Corinne Lelia. *Louisiana Folktales and Songs in French Dialects with Linguistic Notes.* Geo. Peabody, M.A., 1923.

681. Saucier, Corrine Lelia. *Historie et traditions de la paroisse des Avoyelles en Louisiane*. Laval U., Ph.D., 1949. *Pub.*: (in part) under the title *Traditions de la paroisse* . . . . *Memoirs of the American Folklore Society* 47 (Philadelphia, 1956). Pp. vii, 162, bibliog., music.

> Contains approximately sixty chansons, with texts, music and some explanation of the origin of the songs. References to music included in other chapters making up the work.

682. Sauers, Howard Walter. *The Psychological Effects of Music Upon the People of the United States During Wartime*. Pacific, M.A. (music), 1943. Pp. 105.

683. Schaaf, Karlheinz. *Das Volkslied der Donauschwaben; mit besonderer Berücksichtigung des Brauchtumsliedes und des Erzählliedes*. Tübingen (phil.), 1956. Pp. 420, music.

684. Scharnberg, Rudolf. *Volkslied und Volksbildung. Der pädagogische Gehalt der deutschen Volksliedbewegung*. Hamburg (phil.), 1939. *Pub.*: Hamburg, Hansischer Gilden-Verl., 1939. Pp. 128.

685. Schatz, Walter. *Die Zünfte der Spielleute und die Organisation der Orchester-Musiker in Deutschland*. Greifswald (law), 1921. Pp. 27.

686. Scheithauer, Lothar J. *Rhythmus und Volkslied. Ein Beitrag zum methodischen Problem der Rhythmusanalyse*. Leipzig (phil.), 1951 (1952). Pp. 135, xix.

687. Schiffer, Brigitte. *Die Oase Siwa und ihre Musik*. Berlin (phil.), 1936. *Pub.*: Bottrop, W. Postberg [1936?]. Pp. vi, 128, illus., music.

688. Schinhan, Philip. *Die Musik der Papago und Yurok. Ein Beitrag zum Studium der Kultur des Südens und Nordens der Pazifischen Küste*. Vienna (phil.), 1937. Pp. 328.

689. Schmitz, Carl August. *Der Tanz- und Kultplatz in Neu-Guinea und Melanesien. Materialien zur Monographie eines conditionalen Kulturelements*. Cologne (phil.), 1955. *Pub.*: under the title *Der Tanz- u. Kultplatz in Melanesien als Versammlungsort u. mimischer Schauplatz. Die Schaubühne* 46 (Emsdetten, Lechte, 1955). Pp. vii, 184.

690. Schönberg, Jakob. *Die traditionellen Gesänge des israelitischen Gottesdienstes in Deutschland. Musikwissenschaftliche Untersuchung der in A. Baers "Baal T'fillah" gesammelten Synagogengesänge.* Erlangen (phil.), 1925 (1926). Pp. 95.

Considerations of Abraham Baer's work, *Bā'al Tefillah, oder der practische Vorbeten* (1871), an extensive collection of over 1500 Jewish melodies from Germany, Poland and Portugal.

691. Schattner, Hermann Josef. *Volksbildung durch Musikerziehung. Leben und Wirken Hans Georg Nägelis.* Saarbrücken (phil.), 1960. Pp. 398. *Pub.*: Kaiserslautern, Otterbach, 1960.

Nägeli was a Swiss song composer, teacher, writer on musical subjects, music publisher, and founder and president of the Swiss Association for the Cultivation of Music. He did much to improve musical education in the elementary schools, applying and writing several books on the subject of the Pestalozzian system.

692. Schomerus, Lambert. *Das Volkslied Thüringens im Rahmen des gesamtmitteldeutschen Raumes.* Munich (phil.), 1941.

693. Schoolfield, George Clarence. *The Figure of the Musician in German Literature from Romanticism to the Present.* Princeton U., Ph.D. (germ. lit.), 1949. Pp. 436. *D.A.* XV, 829. *Pub.*: *University of No. Car. Studies in the Germanic Languages* 19 (Chapel Hill, U. of No. Car. Press, 1956). Pp. xv, 204.

694. Schopp, Joseph. *Das deutsche Arbeitslied.* Heidelberg (phil.), 1935. *Pub.*: *Germanische Bibliothek* II, 38 (Heidelberg, Winter, 1935). Pp. x, 376.

695. Schubert, Melvin Frank. *An Analysis of Certain Similarities Between the City Dionysia and the Fort Hall Sun Dances.* So. California, M.A., 1954. Pp. 111.

696. Schuessler, Karl. *An Investigation of Musical Taste from the Point of View of Sociology.* Indiana U., Ph.D. (sociol.), 1947. Pp. viii, 145, bibliog., tables.

Data collected in Evansville, Indiana, where musical selections used were presented to over 1200 persons.

697. Schuffenhauer, Gerhart. *Die tschechoslowakische Volksmusik und ihr Einfluss auf die Opern Fr. Smetanas.* Berlin, F.U. (phil.), 1957. Pp. 94, music.

698. Schuhmacher, Wilhelm. *Leben und Seele des deutschen Soldatenlieds im Weltkrieg.* Heidelberg (phil.), 1922. Pp. iv, 326.

699. Scott, Joseph Wright. *The Japanese Noh Play: The Essential Elements in Its Theatre Art Form.* Ohio State U., Ph.D., 1949.

700. Seaman, G. R. *Influence of Folk-Song on Russian Opera Up to the Time of Glinka.* Oxford (Keble), Ph.D., 1962.

701. Seeger, Horst. *Komponist und Folklore in der Musik des 20. Jahrhunderts. Ein Beitrag zur Differenzierung der Musikgeschichte in der Epoche des Imperialismus.* Berlin H.U. (phil.), 1958. Pp. 125, music, tables.

702. Segales, Virginia Jean. *Development of American Folk Music.* Coll.-Conserv. of Music of Cincinnati, M.M., 1947. Pp. 100, bibliog., music.
    Main text gives background and a few musical examples of Indian music; Negro music; sea songs; lumber, railroad and Kentucky mountain songs; cowboy songs; popular songs. Musical examples are found in the appendixes.

703. Seidl, Helmut. *Das Rackett. Ein Beitrag zur Musikinstrumentenkunde.* Leipzig (phil.), 1959. Pp. 76, music.

704. Sellers, William Edward. *The Folklore of Kinship in the British Traditional Ballads.* Boston U., Ph.D. (music), 1956. Pp. 235.

705. Sheffield, Sarah Vantrease. *A Study of Indian Dances.* Geo. Peabody, M.A. (phy. ed.), 1930. Pp. 176, illus., col. pls.
    General study, no specific tribes.

706. Shelton, Austin, J., Jr. *Social Criticism in English and Scotch Folk Ballads.* St. Louis U., Ph.D. (engl. lit.), 1955.

707. Sher, Allen Arthur. *Folk and Square Dancing as Related to the Social Studies Unit in New York City Elementary Schools.* Columbia T.C., Ed.D., 1963. Pp. 494. *D.A.* XXIV, 2774.
    "This project was planned to list and classify folk dances, square dances, and singing games."

708. Sherman, Shirley Biller. *The History of Hebrew and Jewish Music in the Temple and Synagogue.* Northwestern U., M.M., 1949. Pp. vii, 144, bibliog., many music exs.

87

Discusses origins; instruments; manner of performance; prayer and Biblical modes; notation and interpretation; influence of Moorish, troubador and Christian elements; musical decline and reform; famous cantors; the present era.

709. Shlanta, Boghdan A. *A Comparison of Navajo and Pueblo Indians in Musical Talent.* New Mexico, M.A. (psych.), 1938. Pp. viii, 77, tables.
A comparison of talent among children from the 7th to 12th grades using the Seashore *Measure of Musical Talent.* In general, the Pueblos are superior in rhythm and in tonal intensity and rhythm; however, in most measures, the differences are not significant, and change from age to age.

710. Shockett, Bernard Irwin. *A Stylistic Study of the Blues, 1917-1931, as Practiced by Jazz Instrumentalists.* New York U., Ph.D. (music ed.). In process.

711. Shoup, Gail L. *Present Trends in Dance Notation.* California (Los Angeles), M.A. (theatre arts), 1951. Pp. 123, bibliog., illus.
A review of the major systems to 1951; their advantages and disadvantages.

712. Sichardt, Wolfgang. *Der alpenländische Jodler und der Ursprung des Jodelns.* Jena (phil.), 1939. *Pub.: Schriften zur Volksliedkunde u. völkerkundlichen Musikwiss.* 2 (Berlin, Hahnefeld, 1939). Pp. x, 185.

713. Sider, Ronald R. *The Development of Music in Central America.* Eastman, Ph.D. (music theory). In process.

714. Sifuentes, Fernando R. *A Comparative Study of New Mexican and Mexican Popular Songs.* New Mexico, M.A. (mod. lang.), 1940. Pp. 102.

715. Simmins, G. J. P. *A Structural-Functional Analysis of the Ghost Dance Religion of 1890, with Special Reference to the Oglala, Cheyenne and Arapaho.* London (U.C.), M.A., 1951-52.

716. Simon, Heinrich. *Das deutsche geistliche Volkslied als Gut unserer Kultur.* Münster (phil.), 1924. Pp. v, 89.

717. Sims, John Norman. *The Hymnody of the Camp-Meeting Tradition.* Union Theol. Sem., D.S.M., 1960. Pp. 181.

718. Sirola, Bozidar. *Das istrische Volkslied.* Vienna (phil.), 1920. Manuscript.

719. Skinner, Lucille. *Music in the Cultural Life of the Ancient Greeks and Its Historical Significance.* Coll.-Conserv. of Music of Cincinnati, M.A. (music), 1937. Pp. 99, music.
> Greek music connected with mythology, education, religion, poetry, life, drama of the period; its relation to the Western world and the twentieth century.

720. Slaughter, Jay Leon. *The Role of Music in the Mormon Church, School and Life.* Indiana U., D.M.E., 1964. Pp. 404, bibliog., music.
> Beginning with a treatment of the idealogical (sic) basis for music in Mormonism, the author then deals with the music activities which took place under each of the Presidents of the Church from 1830 (Joseph Smith) to the present (David O. Kay). Discussions of Mormon folksongs, music notation, instrumental music, music in schools and at social functions are included.

721. Small, Katharine Lucille. *The Influence of the Gospel Song on the Negro Church.* Ohio State U., M.A. (music), 1945.

722. Smith, Carlton York. *Early Lutheran Hymnody in America, from the Colonial Period to the Year 1850.* So. California, Ph.D. (musicol.), 1956. Pp. xix, 302, facs.

723. Smith, Edna Eveland. *Ceremonials of the Papago and Pima Indians, with Special Emphasis on the Relationship of the Dance to Their Religion.* Iowa, M.A., 1935. Pp. 66.

724. Smith, Edna Marilyn. *Music in West Africa.* Columbia U., Ed.D. (music), 1961. Pp. 221. *D.A.* XXIII, 1383.
> Traces the "general development of music in West Africa, with particular reference to the interaction of tribal societies and the various forces of acculturation which have invaded West Africa especially within the past fifty years."

725. Smith, Hugh L., Jr. *The Literary Manifestation of a Liberal Romanticism in American Jazz.* New Mexico, Ph.D. (lit.), 1955. Pp. 257. *D.A.* XV, 1859.
> The relationships between jazz and the other arts in America are briefly treated in order to show that this music owes to American literature its growing national recognition as an art form. George Washington Cable, Lafcadio Hearn and Mark Twain, as well as other American writers, are discussed.

89

726. Smith, Julia Frances. *Aaron Copland, His Work and Contribution to American Music: A Study of the Development of His Musical Style and an Analysis of the Various Techniques of Writing He Has Employed in His Works.* New York U., Ph.D. (music ed.), 1952. Pp. 664. *D.A.* XIII, 103. *Pub.*: N.Y., Dutton, 1955. Pp. 336.

> One of four sections is devoted to tracing "his style development through three main periods: the French-Jazz, the Abstract, and the American Folksong Periods."

727. Smith, L. Mayne. *Bluegrass Music and Musicians; An Introductory Study of a Musical Style in Its Cultural Context.* Indiana U., M.A. (folkl.), 1964. Pp. iv, 94, bibliog., discog., "List of Recorded Bands," "List of Standard Bluegrass Pieces." *Pub.*: in Xerox form, by the author. To be pub., in part, in the *J. of Amer. Folklore.*

> Describes bluegrass style as a way of performing music and discusses those aspects of its cultural and historical context that seem most responsible for determining the nature of the style.

728. Smith, Robert L. *A Graphic Interpretation of Four Pueblo Indian Corn Dances.* New Mexico, M.A., 1951.

> Illustrated by Smith's paintings. Also 21 plates and 18 photographs of dances, dancers, and costumes. Sia, Santo Domingo, Jémez, San Felipe.

729. Smith, Wilbur Arthur. *A Study of the Use of the English Folk Music Scales in Eleven Selected Symphonies.* So. California, Ph.D. (music), 1956. Pp. 285, illus., music.

> Contains analysis of folksong musical characteristics compared to those of symphonic themes, as well as discussion of harmonic and contrapuntal problems in relation to the folk idiom.

730. Sneed, Adelaide B. *Musical Instruments from Earliest Records to the Year 1 A.D.* Boston U., M.A., 1934. Pp. 64, illus.

> Divided into two parts, the first dealing with musical instruments developed "by the various races," and the second dealing with the development of instruments according to national boundaries including the Assyrians, Hebrews, Greeks, and Chinese.

731. Snow, Ira Jean. *A Study of the Five Civilized Indian Tribes of Oklahoma.* So. California, M.M. (music), 1946. Pp. 349, music.

> Problems of integrating Indian music, along with art, regional history, and English, into the junior high school. Two original transcriptions.

732. Snyder, D. Geraldine. *Seneca Indian Songs.* Northwestern U., M.M., 1944. Pp. 39, bibliog., 10 music exs., scales.

Based on original research. Description of historical background, songs and dances, musical instruments, method, and musical analysis.

733. Sohler, Heinrich. *Beiträge zur Geschichte der Heilmusik.* Berlin (phil.), 1934. Pp. 47.

734. Sorenson, G. N. *Influence of American Life on the Rhythms of the Decorative Arts, Music, and Dancing.* So. California, M.A. (fine arts), 1946. Pp. 171.

Attempts to correlate rhythms of the arts with socio-economic factors and the "spirit of the times" throughout American history.

735. Sorgatz, Heimfried. *Musiker und Musikanten als dichterisches Motiv. Eine Studie zur Auffassung und Gestaltung des Musikers in der erzählenden Dichtung vom Sturm und Drang bis zum Realismus.* Marburg (phil.), 1939. *Pub.: Literarhist.-musikwiss. Abhandlungen* 6 (Würzburg, Triltsch, 1939). Pp. xv, 133.

736. Spassoff, Wassil. *Volksmusik, Musikinstrumente und Tänze der Bulgaren.* Vienna (phil.), 1931.

737. Spector, Johanna L. *A Comparative Study of Scriptural Cantilation and Accentuation: Pentatuch.* Hebrew Union Coll., Ph.D. (music), 1950. Pp. iii, 193, bibliog., music, 3 tables.

Deals with a history of cantilation, cheironomy, biblical cantilation and temple rites, types, and notation in Jewish, Masoretic, Babylonian, Tiberian traditions; with the functional significance of three groups of accents and tables of Ta'amin grammarians; and compares Babylonian and Yemenite accents.

738. Spell, Lota May Harrigan. *Musical Education in North America During the Sixteenth and Seventeenth Centuries.* Texas, Ph.D. (educa.), 1923. Pp. 127, map, 11 plates.

Deals primarily with Spanish and French influences, but includes Indian musical training.

739. Spencer, Katherine. *Mythology and Values: An Analysis of Navaho Chantway Myths.* Chicago, Ph.D. (anthro.), 1952. Pp. 349. *Pub.: Memoirs of the American Folklore Soc.* 48 (Phila., 1957). Pp. ix, 240, bibliog., charts.

Incidental references to song and dance.

740. Spiegel, Walter. *Die Bedeutung der Musik für die griechische Erziehung im klassischen Altertum.* Erlangen (phil.), 1910. *Pub.*: Berlin, Warneck, 1910. Pp. 92.

741. Spier, Leslie. *The Sun Dance of the Plains Indians: Its Development and Diffusion.* Columbia U., Ph.D. (anthro.), 1920. Pp. i, 76, bibliog., front., graphs, map, vita. *Pub.*: Amer. Museum of Nat. Hist., *Anthro. Papers* 14 (1921), pp. 451-527.

> Description of Sun Dance complex in detail, organization and procedures, historic relations, diffusion and assimilation.

742. Spieser, Fritz. *Das Leben des Volksliedes im Rahmen eines Lothringerdorfes (Hambach, Kr. Saargemünd).* Marburg (phil.), 1934. *Pub.: Bausteine zur Volkskunde und Religionswiss.* 8 (Bühl-Baden, Konkordia, 1934). Pp. 153.

743. Springer, Hermann. *Das altprovenzalische Klagelied.* Berlin (phil.), 1894. *Pub.: Berliner Beitr. zur germanischen und romanischen Philologie* VII, 2 (Berlin, C. Vogt, 1895). Pp. 112.

744. Spurrier, Joseph Howard. *A History of School Music in the Hawaiian Islands to 1950.* Utah State U., D.Ed., 1963. Pp. 509, bibliog. (pp. 463-509), tables.

> The first part is entitled "Indigenous Music Education" and includes a discussion of the ancient culture, the hula halau, and the cultural decline which leads into the second part, concerning music education in the Missionary Period. Part three traces the story of public school music in the Hawaiian Kingdom, while the final part explores school music in the present century.

745. Staab, *Sister* Mary Theresine. *Indian Lullabies; An Analytical Study of Some North American Cradle Songs.* Catholic U., M.A. (music), 1940. Pp. 28, tables.

> An analysis of twenty-one Indian lullabies belonging to fourteen different tribes. The analysis is made of general features such as tonality, harmonic and melodic structure, and rhythmic patterns.

746. Stackhouse, Margaret Elise. *A Study of the American Composer's Stylistic Use of the Folk-Song "Black is the Color of My True Love's Hair."* Eastman, M.A. (music theory), 1956. Pp. iv, 130, music.

> The author traces the use of this particular folksong as a basis for artistic composition by certain twentieth century American composers. The appendix gives additional sources of the song.

747. Stanton, Royal Waltz. *The Quality of Permanence in Protestant Hymn Tunes.* California (Los Angeles), M.A. (music), 1946. Pp. 99, bibliog., music.

A musical analysis indicating that standard tunes did not change greatly though widespread among the folk.

748. Starin, Lorney Gerald. *Music of South American Indians.* Northwestern U., M.M., 1954. Pp. vi, 45, bibliog., 12 figs., music.

Very general report on music of Araucanians, Brazil, Argentina, Peru, Bolivia, Ecuador, and the Inca.

749. Starkey, Virginia. *The Music of the Vikings and Norwegian Composers.* Ohio State U., M.A. (music), 1938.

750. Staudinger, Hans. *Entwicklung und Form der musikalisch-geselligen Organisation.* Heidelberg (phil.), 1913. Pp. 39. *Pub.*: under the title "Individuum und Gemeinschaft in der Kulturorganisation des Vereins," *Schriften zur Soziologie der Kultur* 1 (Jena, Diederichs, 1913). Pp. vi, 174.

751. Stebbins, Robert Alan. *The Minneapolis Jazz Community: The Conflict Between Musical and Commercial Values.* Minnesota, M.A. (sociol.), 1962. Pp. iii, 87, bibliog., tables. Summary in Minn. Acad. of Science *Proceedings* 30 (1962), pp. 75-79.

Fifteen commercial and fifteen jazz musicians were interviewed to test four hypotheses concerned with tensions that develop between practical and aesthetic requirements which emerge in the field of jazz. Most of the major hypotheses were confirmed.

752. Stebbins, Robert Alan. *The Jazz Community: The Sociology of a Musical Sub-culture.* Minnesota, Ph.D. (sociol.), 1964. Pp. 16, 242, 25, maps, tables.

An expansion of the above using twenty five musicians from each group. Two major hypotheses of the study were that jazz musicians rank lower on the larger community variables of class, status and power that do commercial musicians, and, at the same time, that they are higher on these variables when applied to the specialized community of jazz musicians. The hypotheses were largely confirmed.

753. Steed, Thursa. *The Contribution of Russians to the Dance.* Geo. Peabody, M.A. (phy. ed.), 1934. Pp. 91.

754. Stegemeier, Henri Gustave. *The Dance of Death in Folk Song.* Chicago, Ph.D. (germ. lit.), 1939. Pp. 231. Lithographed.

755. Stephan, Waltraut. *Die Haltung Freier Mut und das älteste Volkslied. Studien zum Wandel vom ritterlich-höfischen zum bürgerlichen Mittelalter.* Bonn (phil.), 1938. *Pub.*: Würzburg, Triltsch, 1938. Pp. 154.

756. Stephani, Reinhart. *Die deutsche musikalische Jungendbewegung.* Marburg (phil.), 1952. Pp. 413, vi.

757. Stevens, Nadia Mihailovska (Mrs.). *Some Aspects of the Bulgarian Folk Music.* Boston U., M.A. (music), 1937. Pp. 57, music, texts.

> The study attempts to trace the origin of Bulgarian folk music with its lyric, and to show how it has kept its unifying qualities so as to remain uniquely Bulgarian. Topics include an historical sketch, lyrics, rhythm, dancing, instruments, intervals, harmony, and scales.

758. Steward, Julian H. *Tambourines and Shamanism.* California, M.A., 1926.

759. Stewart, Iva May. *A Study of Music in the Negro Secondary Schools of Houston, Texas.* Iowa, M.A. (music), 1943.

760. Stewart, Rebecca Marie. *An Examination of the Banāras School of Tabla Performance.* Hawaii, M.A. (music), 1965. Pp. v, 154, bibliog., 25 photos, transcription of drum mnemonics, *bols* in Devanāgari and transliteration, index. A demonstration tape recording, *Tāl Bols* and *Tāl Thekās*, 15′ 20″, and *Tāl Prastārs*, 14′ 00″, deposited separately.

> The study presents the historical development of North Indian rhythmic concepts, historical development and physical construction of the drum, musical elements of performance, schools of performance, course of instruction at Banāras Hindu University, transcription by *bol* names with indication of rhythm, and analysis of *tāl bols, tāl thekās* and *tāl prastārs.*

761. Stockmann, Doris. *Der Volksgesang in der Altmark von 1850 bis zur Gegenwart. Eine volkskundlich-musikhistorische Untersuchung.* Berlin, H.U. (phil.), 1958. Pp. ix, 501.

762. Stöhr, Maria. *Beiträge zur vorgeschichtlichen Instrumentenkunde der ägäisch-vorderasiatischen Kulturwelt.* Vienna (phil.), 1936.

94

763. Stone, Yona. *Music and History in Ancient Greece.* Coll.-Conserv. of Music of Cincinnati, M.M., 1951. Pp. 34, bibliog., music.

> Purpose of the thesis is to determine the effect of Greek history on Greek music. Discusses prehistoric, classical, post-classical periods. No footnote references.

764. Stranlund, Virginia K. *Swedish Folk Music and Dancing; Its Use in the American Classroom.* So. California, M.M., 1950. Pp. 301, illus., music.

> Lists dances, costumes, names of festivals, and standard pieces; recommendations for suitable pieces at each school level.

765. Strnad, Waltraud. *Untersuchungen zum Melodiebildungsvermögen des Volksschulkindes.* Erlangen (phil.), 1952 (1953). Pp. 109.

766. Struckman, Robert Powers. *"Sun Dance" and Other Stories.* Montana State U., M.A., 1947. Pp. 134.

> Assiniboine, Gros Ventre fiction, based on authentic dance and setting.

767. Sugihara, Setsuko. *Ceremonial Music of Japan.* Pacific, M.A. (music), 1954. Pp. 224.

768. Swan, Clara Le Grande. *A Collection of Ballads and Folk Songs from Morning Sun, Iowa.* Iowa, M.A. (engl.), 1929. Pp. iii, 178.

> Texts only, collected by the author.

769. Sweeney, Cecily Pauline. *The Piano Music of Carlos Chavez.* California (Los Angeles), M.A. (music), 1957. Pp. 81.

> Traces Chavez's development including his times of preoccupation with authentic Mexican music.

770. Sypniewski, Jan. *Ein Problem der Gegenwartsmusik: Jazz, unter besonderer Berücksichtigung des symphonischen Jazz (George Gershwin).* Zürich (phil.), 1949. Pp. 205.

771. Tack, Melva Pauline. *Typical Spanish Folk Songs of North New Mexico Adapted and Arranged for Use in a Program of Music Education.* Kansas, M.A. (music ed.), 1948. Pp. 91.

772. Tanner, Paul O. *A Technical Analysis of the Development of Jazz.* California (Los Angeles), M.A., 1962.

773. Taut, Kurt. *Beiträge zur Geschichte der Jagdmusik.* Leipzig (phil.), 1926 (1927). *Pub.*: under the title *Die Anfänge der Jagdmusik.* Leipzig, Selbstverl., 1927. Pp. 190.

774. Tax, Sol. *Primitive Social Organization with Some Description of the Social Organization of the Fox Indians.* Chicago, Ph.D. (anthro.), 1935. Pp. 212, bibliog., maps, tables. *Pub.*: (in part) under the title "The Social Organization of the Fox Indians." In: *Social Anthropology of North American Tribes.* Presented to Prof. A. R. Radcliffe-Brown . . . by Fred Eggan, *ed.*, and others (Chicago, Univ. of Chicago Press, 1937), pp. 241-282.

> Appendix V, "A brief description of the Peyote cult among the Fox Indians;" Appendix VI, "An account of the ceremonial runners of the Fox Indians," contain material on singing and drumming in ceremonial rites. No songs are given.

775. Taylor, Vernon Husson. *Contrapuntal Techniques in the Music of Béla Bartók.* Northwestern U., Ph.D. (music), 1950. Pp. 318, bibliog., music.

> Contains chapters on Bartók's life; rhythm, meter, and tempo; melodic style; simultaneous melodic lines; structure and form; durational distribution of tone. Uses analytical method in part from ethnomusicology.

776. Tchen, Ysia. *La Musique chinoise en France au XVIIIe siècle.* Paris, thèse lettres, 1948.

777. Termini, Olga A. *German Folk Song for the Seventh or Eighth Grade General Music Class.* So. California, M.M., 1957. Pp. 301, music.

> Evaluates German songs in the light of teaching, and attempts to enlarge the selection for better coverage and to provide background information for teachers.

778. Tesack, Kathryn Elizabeth. *A Study of the Oldest Hawaiian Music Culture and a Plan for Its Utilization in the High School Music Courses of That Territory.* Washington, M.A. (music ed.), 1932. Pp. iv, 92, bibliog.

> Includes the notation of 23 Hawaiian songs of the old tradition, sung by school children and old people visited by the author. Also includes a brief description of modern Hawaiian music and musical instruments. Only those melodies are presented that could be used in school glee clubs and similar organizations. No analysis.

779. Thielecke, Richard. *Die soziale Lage der Berufsmusiker in Deutschland und die Entstehung, Entwicklung und Bedeutung ihrer Organisationen.* Frankfurt a.M. (econ. and sociol.), 1922. Pp. xv, 313.

780. Thieme, Darius L. *A Selected Bibliography of Periodical Articles on the Music of the Native Peoples of Sub-Saharan Africa.* Catholic U., M.S. (lib. sci.), 1963. *Pub.: African Music* (Wash., D.C., Library of Congress, Reference Department, Music Division, 1964). Pp. xxvi, 54, map, indexes.

781. Thomas, Virginia M. *Nationalistic Traits in Russian Music, Derived from an Analysis of Russian Folk-Song Compositions of the "Russian Five."* Syracuse U., M.A. (music), 1942. Pp. 81.

782. Thompson, Jean Graham. *China and Her Music.* Northwestern U., M.M., 1947. Pp. iii, 108, bibliog., illus.
Includes history of China and Chinese music; instruments and their music; Chinese religion and philosophy.

783. Thompson, Merle. *Ohio Composers of Popular Music.* Northwestern U., M.M., 1942.

784. Thorpe, Alice Louise. *American Songsters of the Eighteenth Century.* Brown U., M.A. (engl.), 1935. Pp. 365.
Definition and list of titles with dates. Indexes: first lines; according to author; according to type (e.g., amatory, amatory-facetious, amatory-military, and so forth). Bibliogs.: American songsters; books consulted.

785. Thrower, Sarah Selina. *The Spiritual of the Gullah Negro in South Carolina.* Coll.-Conserv. of Music of Cincinnati, M.M., 1954. Pp. 64, bibliog., music.
Definition and origin of the spiritual, peculiarities of the Gullah spiritual, presentation and performance of spirituals.

786. Tibbets, Edith MacKerricher. *The Development of Mexican Music.* Pacific, M.A. (music), 1936. Pp. 281.

787. Tinsley, Vallie. *Some Negro Songs Heard on the Hills of North Louisiana.* Louisiana State U., M.A., 1928.

788. Tiplady, Eleanor. *The Music of China, History, Scales, Instruments.* Coll.-Conserv. of Music of Cincinnati, M.M., 1946. Pp. 96, bibliog., music.
Concerns Chinese ideas on music, musical scales, musical instruments, and pentatonic scales of other nations.

789. Tischer, Gerhard. *Die aristotelischen Musikprobleme.* Berlin (phil.), 1902. Pp. 34. *Pub.: Musikwiss. Studien* 3 (Berlin, Ebering, 1903). Pp. 100.

790. Tocus, Clarence Spencer. *The Negro Idiom in American Musical Composition.* So. California, M.A. (music), 1942. Pp. 143.

791. Tolle, Wilhelm. *Grundformen des reformatorischen Schulliederbuches vorwiegend um 1600.* Halle (phil.), 1935 (1936). *Pub.:* Wolfenbüttel, Kallmeyer, 1936. Pp. viii, 163.

792. Townsend, A. O. *The American Folk-Song and Its Influence on the Works of American Composers.* So. California, A.M. (music), 1938. Pp. 116, bibliog.
   Traces sources of American folksong and influence, reaching the conclusion that the Negro influence has been the strongest.

793. Trantham, Carrie Pool. *An Investigation of the Unpublished Negro Folk Songs of Dorothy Scarborough.* Baylor U., M.A. (engl.), 1941. Pp. 280.
   In two divisions, treating secular songs and religious ballads. Includes notes which Miss Scarborough made on the texts.

794. Treder, Dorothea. *Die Musikinstrumente in den höfischen Epen der Blütezeit.* Greifswald (phil.), 1933. *Pub.:* Greifswald, Bamberg, 1933. Pp. 57.

795. Trexevant, Adlee Houston. *A Comparative Survey of Music in the Larger Negro High Schools of Texas.* Northwestern U., M.M., 1948.

796. Trimillos, Picardo Diosdado. *Some Social and Musical Aspects of the Music of the Taosug in Sulu, Philippines.* Hawaii, M.A. (music), 1965. Pp. v, 200, bibliog., 46 pp. music, 12 tables, texts with translation, glossary. A tape recording, 14′ 50″, is deposited separately.
   Based on field work in Sulu in 1963, this study provides an ethnographic analysis of the context of music in Taosug life, seven *Baat* in double transcription (one giving the general outline, the other providing a higher level of specificity of the performance style, especially the details of vocal ornamentation), and an analysis of their musical content.

797. Trone, Dolly G. *The Influence of the World War (1917) on the Art of Music in America.* Northwestern U., M.M., 1940.

798. Tsukazaki, Doris Takesue. *The Place of Hawaiian Songs in Public School Music*. Eastman, M.A. (music ed.), 1945. Pp. iii, 69, music.

> The educational, sociological, and musical values of Hawaiian music are discussed, together with selected songs suitable for presentation in the curriculum of the American public school.

799. Turechek, Alma Alice. *Problems Involved in Arranging a Selected Group of Czech Folk Songs for Educational Purposes*. Iowa, M.A., 1941. Pp. 45.

800. Turpen, Charles. *Music in Navaho Ceremonialism*. Coll.-Conserv. of Music of Cincinnati, M.M., 1951. Pp. 91, bibliog., music.

> In three sections: The Music and Religion of the Navaho, the Rites of the Night Way, and a supplement containing the translations of the prayer for the ninth night of the Night Way and the Hastsehogan Bigin myth, as well as three groups of music transcriptions of songs from the Night Way.

801. Tyer, Mona Gross. *A Study of the Children's Song Literature of Latin America Including a Collection of Songs from the Countries of South America and Mexico; Also a Survey of the Cultural Background of These Countries*. Colorado S.C. of Ed., M.A. (music), 1942. Pp. 151.

802. Ursule, *Sister* Marie. *La civilisation traditionnelle des Lavalois*. Ph.D., Laval, 1951(?). *Pub.: Les Archives de Folklore* 5-6 (Quebec, Les Presses Universitaires Laval, 1951). Pp. 403, bibliog., illus., map, music.

> Indicates those traditions still living and those lost, as taken from oral sources, and manuscript and printed records. Chapter III, "Oral Traditions," includes 115 chansons.

803. Uyehara, Yokuo. *Historical Development of the Kabuki Since the Meiji Restoration*. Hawaii, M.A., 1936.

804. Vaughan, Portia Loyetta. *An Investigation of Music as Taught in a Government Indian School in Oklahoma*. Kansas, M.A., 1939. Pp. 189, bibliog., 8 photos, tables.

> A discussion of the music of the Indian of the past and present is followed by a study of the organization of music courses taught at Sequoyah Indian School at Tahlequah, Oklahoma. Results of questionnaires sent to eleven other Indian Service schools are tabulated. A list of ten specific suggestions for improvement is included.

805. Velimirović, Miloš Milorad. *The Byzantine Elements in Early Slavonic Chant.* Harvard, Ph.D. (music), 1957. Vol. 1: pp. 396, text; Vol. II: pp. cxxv, 64, appendixes and plates.

806. Voget, Frederick William. *The Diffusion of the Wind River Shoshone Sun-Dance to the Crow Indians of Montana.* Yale U., Ph.D. (anthro.), 1948. *Pub.:* (summary) *Amer. Anthro.* 50 (1948), pp. 634-646, map.
> A brief history of "the diffusion and a description of the roles and motives of the individuals directly responsible for the transmission of the Shoshone ceremonial." Based on field work in 1941 and 1946.

807. Voigt, Eberhard. *Die Music-Hall Songs und das öffentliche Leben Englands.* Greifswald (phil.), 1929. Pp. 191.

808. Von Haupt, Lois. *Jazz; An Historical and Analytical Study.* New York U., M.A. (music), 1945. Pp. 131.

809. Von Wenck, Katherine. *A Critical Evaluation of Czechoslovakian Folk Dances for Use in American School Situations.* New York U., M.A. (phy. ed.), 1933. Pp. 123.

810. Wängler, Hans-Heinrich. *Homogenisierungsprobleme zu musikalischen Beispielen aus Süd-Ost-Neuguinea.* Hamburg (phil.), 1949. Pp. 73.

811. Walden, Jean Elizabeth. *The History, Development, and Contribution of the Negro Folk Song.* Northwestern U., M.M., 1945. Pp. 75, bibliog., music.
> General information on early history, white influence, and analytical characteristics. Discusses religious and social songs with examples, blues, music in war service, Negro musicians and the Negro song, later white influence on Negro song.

812. Waldrop, Rebecca. *Sacred, Classic, Court and Ritual Dances of the Far East.* Geo. Peabody, M.A. (phy. ed.), 1935. Pp. 152.

813. Walker, Andrew J. *Popular Songs and Ballads in English Drama.* Harvard, Ph.D., 1934.

814. Wallner, Franz. *Das Musikalisch-Volkstümliche im deutschen weltlichen Lied des 17. Jahrhunderts.* Erlangen (phil.), 1925. Pp. 213.

815. Walters, William R. *A Study of the Nature and Scope of Christian Judgment Service Music.* Western Reserve U., Ph.D. (musicol.), 1963.

816. Walton, Edna Lou. *Navaho Traditional Poetry.* California, Ph.D., 1921. *Pub.*: "American Indian Poetry," *Amer. Anthro.* 27 (1925), pp. 25-52; "Navajo Song Patterning," *J. of Amer. Folklore* 43 (1930), pp. 105-118.

817. Waltz, Heinrich. *Die Lage der Orchestermusiker in Deutschland mit besonderer Berücksichtigung der Musikgeschäfte ("Stadtpfeifereien").* Heidelberg (phil.), 1906. *Pub.*: *Volkswirtschaftliche Abhandlungen der Badischen Hochschulen* 8 (Karlsruhe, C. Braun, 1906). Pp. vii, 125.

818. Wang, Kwang-chi. *Über die chinesische klassische Oper.* Bonn (phil.), 1934. *Pub.*: *Orient et Occident* 1 (1934), no. 1, pp. 9-21; no. 2, pp. 16-33; no. 3, pp. 13-29.

819. Ware, Luella Catharine (Mrs.). *Songs of the Mono.* Pacific, M.A. (music) [1959?].
   Songs collected from two Mono informants, including a funeral pow-wow and songs about birds, animals, ghosts, stars, hunting and legends.

820. Waschek, Brownlee. *A Study of Czechoslovak Folk Music Transplanted to the Community of Masaryktown, Florida.* Florida State U., M.A. (music ed.), 1959.

821. Waterman, Lucy Ely. *Musical Instruments in Spanish Romanesque Iconography.* New York U., M.A., 1941. Pp. 81.

822. Waterman, Richard Alan. *African Patterns in Trinidad Negro Music.* Northwestern U., Ph.D. (anthro.), 1943. Pp. viii, 261, bibliog., 47 music transcriptions, analyses of tonal structure, 15 tables and charts.
   Analyzes retention of African patterns in Trinidad music, with chapters on the relevant literature, historic contacts of the Negroes of Trinidad, analysis of the music, and comparison of Trinidad music with other historically related styles.

823. Watson, Jack McLaurin. *Negro Folk Music in Eastern South Carolina.* South Carolina, M.A. (music), 1940. Pp. 85.

824. Watson, Karl B. *An Experimental Study of Musical Meanings.* Duke U., Ph.D. (educa.), 1939. Pp. 163. Summary, under the title "The Nature and Measurement of Musical Meaning," in *Psychol. Monographs* 54 (1942).

825. Waugh, Viola Opal. *A Comparison of Various Phases of Modern and Oriental Dances.* Iowa, M.A. (phy. ed.), 1938.

826. Weight, Newell Bryan. *An Historical Study of the Origin and Character of Indigenous Hymn Tunes of the Latter-Day Saints.* So. California, Ph.D. (music), 1961. Pp. 465. D.A. XXII, 3224.
   Mormon hymnology from 1830 to present.

827. Weishaar, Ada Louise. *A Study of the Music of the American Indian.* Coll.-Conserv. of Music of Cincinnati, M.A. (music), 1946. Pp. 63, bibliog., illus., music.
   Beginning with the early history of dance and music, the thesis covers the religious and emotional basis of Indian music, and describes its characteristics and types. Concludes with American composers who write in the Indian idiom.

828. Wellek, Albert. *Typologie der Musikbegabung im deutschen Volke. Grundlegung einer psychologischen Theorie der Musik und Musikgeschichte. (Mit allgemein-psychologischen Beiträgen zur "Tonhöhen"-Unterschiedsempfindlichkeit.)* Leipzig (HabSchr.), 1938. *Pub.: Arbeiten zur Entwicklungspsychologie* 20 (Munich, C. H. Beck, 1939). Pp. xi, 307.

829. Wells, Willie Scruggs. *Indian Music and Its Place in the Curriculum of the Modern School.* West Texas S.C., M.A., 1952. Pp. 100, 8 tables, 8 pls.
   Discusses the background and general characteristics of Indian ceremonies, the work of ethnologists in securing original transcriptions of Indian music, and includes an analysis of a selected group of Indian songs. Characteristics of Indian music are given and the educational importance of Indian music noted.

830. Welty, Frederick Arthur. *Changing Emphasis of Music in the Bible.* Pittsburgh, M.A., 1936. Pp. 49.

831. Wenker, Jerome. *A Computational Method for the Analysis of Anglo-American Folksongs.* Indiana U., M.A. (folkl.), 1964. Pp. vii, 271, bibliog.
   Devoted to the analysis and design of a character music notation which can represent unambiguously the symbols used in symbolic music notation and which is specifically designed for use by the computer.

102

832. Westby, David Leroy. *The Social Organization of a Symphony Orchestra, with Special Attention to the Informal Associations of Symphony Members.* Minnesota, M.A. (sociol.), 1957. Pp. 108, bibliog., graphs, tables.

> The study concerns itself "with problems of mobility, status, leadership . . ." and "with elements of the work situation that arrange the pattern of interaction, or association, of the musicians off the job."

833. Westerhoff, Gerhard. *Christlich-religiöse Züge in den englischschottischen Volksballaden und ihren nordamerikanischen Fassungen.* Bonn, 1942.

834. Weyland, Rudolph Harry. *A Study of the Musical Talent Among Indian Children from the Pawnee Indian Agency Jurisdiction, Pawnee, Oklahoma.* Oklahoma State U., M.S., 1945. Pp. 56, 16 tables.

> A study of musical talent by means of the Seashore *Measures of Musical Talent* among 260 Pawnee, Ponca and Otoe children. Results indicate a wide range of difference between Indian children and Seashore norms for heterogeneous groups of white children, although there is strong indication that such differences become less as the Indian children receive further education. It is possible that the difference would be slight or cease to exist under matched and equal environmental conditions from birth.

835. Whaples, Miriam Karpilow. *Exoticism in Dramatic Music, 1600-1800.* Indiana U., Ph.D. (music), 1958. Pp. v, 415, bibliog., index, music.

> Several chapters are devoted to Turkish music, the music of the peoples of the Far East, chiefly China, and the music of nonliterate peoples of Latin America, Indians of North America, Africa and Oceania. Three appendixes (120 pp.) present excerpted references to music and dance and music examples as cited in the accounts of travelers and voyagers visiting the above-mentioned areas, from the earliest western contact to 1800.

836. Wheeler, Mary. *Ohio River Songs of the Packet-Boat Era.* Coll.-Conserv. of Music of Cincinnati, M.A. (music), 1937. Pp. 164, bibliog., music.

> Consists almost entirely of 68 music examples which are given melodically, textually, and analyzed very briefly as to scale. Background of most examples given.

837. White, Lillian O. *The Folksongs of the American Negro and Their Value Today.* Idaho, M.A., 1925.

838. Wiant, Bliss Mitchell. *Possibilities of Polyphonic Treatment of Chinese Tunes.* Boston U., M.A., 1936. Pp. ii, 56, music.

839. Wiant, Bliss Mitchell. *The Character and Function of Music in Chinese Culture.* Geo. Peabody, Ph.D. (music), 1946. Pp. vii, 325. *Pub.*: Geo. Peabody, *Contribs. to Educa.*, No. 376.
An investigation into "how music has played and is playing an unusual part in the political, literary, social, religious and everyday life of the Chinese people."

840. Wieschhoff, Heinz. *Die afrikanischen Trommeln und ihre ausserafrikanischen Beziehungen.* Frankfurt a.M. (phil.), 1933. *Pub.*: *Studien zur Kulturkunde* 2 (Stuttgart, Strecker u. Schröder, 1933). Pp. vii, 148.

841. Wike, Joyce Annabel. *Modern Spirit Dancing of Northern Puget Sound.* Washington, M.A., 1941. Pp. 145.

842. Wilder, Carleton S. *The Yaqui Deer Dance; A Study in Cultural Change.* Arizona, M.A. (anthro.), 1940. Pp. 157, music.
An examination of the deculturation of the Deer Dance as performed at Pascua village, near Tucson, Arizona. Includes examination of form and content of twenty songs sung during the dance.

843. Wilgus, Donald Knight. *A Catalog of American Folk Songs on Commercial Records.* Ohio State U., M.A., 1947.

844. Wilgus, Donald Knight. *A History of Anglo-American Ballad Scholarship Since 1898.* Ohio State U., Ph.D. (engl. lit.), 1954. 2 vols. Pp. 519. *D.A.* XV, 1366. *Pub.*: New Brunswick, N.J., Rutgers Univ. Press, 1959. Pp. xx, 446, bibliog., discog.
Deals with three fields of scholarship: the dispute over origins; the collection and publication of all varieties of orally transmitted song; the historical and critical study of folksongs. "The Negro-White Spiritual" is discussed in an appendix.

845. Williams, Dalton D. *The Status of Music in Rural Negro Schools of Clay County, Mississippi.* Northwestern U., M.M., 1955.

846. Williams, Frances Sellers. *American Dances for the American Secondary Schools.* Temple U., M.A. (phy. ed.), 1933. Pp. 184.
Dances of the American Indian along the frontier, with some mention of the Blackfoot, Makah, Pueblo. Also Algonquin and Sioux dances.

847. Williams, James R. *Tribal Education of the Hopi Indian Child.* Arizona S.C., M.A. (educa.), 1948. Pp. 99, music, pls.

Thesis includes five Hopi songs learned early in childhood. Deals primarily with education and history, as well as ceremonies, initiations, folktales and music in words and dances.

848. Williams, Thelma A. *Origin and Analysis of Negro Folk-Song.* Wayne State U., M.S. (music), 1938. Pp. 68, music, tables.

A very general sketch of Negro folk music in the United States, using older methods and sources. The emphasis is decidedly emotional-sentimental.

849. Wilson, James Reginald. *Ballad Tunes of the Miramichi.* New York U., M.A., 1961. Pp. 148, bibliog., charts, music.

Concerned with part of a large collection of folk tunes obtained by the author and Dr. Louise Manny in the Miramichi Valley of New Brunswick, Canada, over the past twelve years.

850. Winter, Elizabeth Harrell. *Music in Texas Since 1920.* Sul Ross S.C., M.A., 1940. Pp. 43.

The historical background of music in Texas prior to 1920 reveals the influence upon music of outside ethnic groups as each occupied Texas. Includes a chapter on "The Texas Indian and Music."

851. Wiora, Walter. *Die Variantenbildung im Volkslied. Ein Beitrag zur systematischen Musikwissenschaft.* Freiburg i. Br. (phil.), 1937. *Pub.:* (in part) under the title "Systematik der musikalischen Erscheinungen des Umsingens." In: *Jahrb. für Volksliedforschung* 7 (Berlin, 1941), pp. 128-195. As a separate, with 69 additional pages, *Schriften zur musikal. Volks- u. Rassenkunde* 4 (Wolfenbüttel, Kallmeyer, 1940). Pp. v, 128.

852. Witherson, Maude I. *Effects of Race and Nationality Upon Music Measurement.* Syracuse U., M.A., 1935.

853. Witthoft, John. *Green Corn Ceremonialism in the Eastern Woodlands.* Pennsylvania, M.A. (anthro.), 1946. *Pub.:* Univ. of Mich., Mus. of Anthrop., *Occas. Contrs.,* No. 13 (1949). Pp. 91, bibliog., tables.

A detailed survey of the Green Corn Dance, its distribution, similarities and differences between various areas, evidences of historical connection, and musical modifications and differences in function as found in the different ethnic groups. Also studies the distribution of Corn Mother myths and some possible relationships between these tales and the ceremony. Algonkian, Iroquois, Cherokee, Southeastern Siouan, Creek.

854. Wittrock, Wolfgang. *Die ältesten Typen in der Melodik des ostdeutschen Volksgesanges.* Kiel (phil.), 1963. Pp. 257, bibliog., music.

855. Wolf, Edward Christopher. *Lutheran Church Music in America During the Eighteenth and Early Nineteenth Centuries.* Illinois, Ph.D. (music), 1960. Pp. 473. D.A. XXI, 3118.
Points out the considerable emphasis which was placed on music and singing and which, collectively, "had an important influence upon the development of early American attitudes toward music."

856. Wolf, R. E. *Style and Function, Constants in the Changing Aesthetics of Musical Expressivity.* Liège, Ph.D., 1954.

857. Wolz, Carl. *Bugaku: Japanese Court Dances, With the Notation of Basic Movements and of Nasori.* Hawaii, M.A. (asian studies), 1965. Pp. vi, 217; 49 figures.
A study of context and content; labanotation scores.

858. Wragg, Eleanor Newton. *The American Civil War Era as Reflected in the Religious Song of the Age.* Boston U., M.A., 1935. Pp. ii, 148, bibliog., "Table of Hymns Considered in This Work."

859. Wright, LeRoy Evert. *The Place of Music in Worship. (The Physical and Psychological Justification of Music in the Worship Experience in the Protestant Churches of America.)* Northwestern U., Ph.D. (music), 1949.

860. Wu, Hoseah. *Some Theoretical Aspects of Chinese Music.* Northwestern U., M.M., 1954.

861. Wünsch, Walther. *Die Geigentechnik der jugoslawischen Guslaren.* Prague (phil.), 1933. *Pub.: Veroff. des musikwiss. Instituts der Deutschen Universität in Prag* 5 (Brünn, Rohrer, 1934). Pp. 60

862. Wyatt, P. J. *I'm Not Selling Anything: Some Folklore from Kansas.* Indiana U., A.M. (folkl.), 1956. Pp. iii, 178, bibliog., photos, transcriptions of songs.
Deals with general folklore study of a county in Kansas.

863. Yamamoto, S. *A Historical Study on the Harp, from the Ancient Orient to Mediaeval Europe.* Tokyo U. Arts, 1957.

864. Yoder, Paul Marvin. *Nineteenth Century Sacred Music of the Mennonite Church in the United States.* Florida State U., Ph.D. (music), 1961. Pp. 188. *D.A.* XXII, 1207.

The purpose of the study was to establish factors affecting the music and to indicate the influences of these factors as they are reflected in the music. An appendix includes a chronological listing of the Mennonite hymnbooks through the various editions from 1742 to 1960.

865. Yoshimura, Y. *The Zither Family in East Asia.* Tokyo U. Arts, 1961.

866. Yost, Ada Martha. *Surviving Folk Ceremonials Among the Shoshone Indians at Fort Hall.* Idaho, M.A., 1932. Pp. 65.

867. Young, Margaret Hershey. *Japanese Kabuki Drama: The History and Meaning of the Essential Elements of Its Theatre Art Form.* Indiana U., Ph.D. (speech and theatre), 1953. Pp. xii, 343, bibliog., glossary.

There are chapters on the background of Kabuki, its origin and development (1596-1750), maturity (1751-1829), decline (1830-1911), and contemporary Kabuki (1912-1953). Music is mentioned throughout, and there is included a section on dance and music. Appendixes: Japanese and Western Chronology; Kabuki Actors, Deceased and Living; [synopses of] Kabuki Plays; Glossary of Kabuki Terms.

868. Young, Robert H. *The History of Baptist Hymnody in England from 1612 to 1800.* So. California, D.M.A., 1959. Pp. 252, bibliog., chart. *D.A.* XX, 1822.

Discusses attitudes of the church founders toward hymn singing, and the spread of texts and tunes in England and America.

869. Young, Russell Scott. *Vieilles chansons de Nouvelle France.* Laval U., Ph.D. [1956?] *Pub.: Les Archives de Folklore* 7 (Quebec, Presses Universitaires Laval, 1956). Pp. 129, illus., music.

The author presents 50 Quebec versions of some 700 French-Canadian folksongs he has collected and deposited in the National Museum of Canada and the Archives of Folklore at Laval University. In a separate section the singer and the place of recording is indicated for each song.

870. Youngblood, Joseph Edward. *Music and Language; Some Related Analytical Techniques.* Indiana U., Ph.D. (music), 1960. Pp. 135. *D.A.* XXI, 2743.

Procedures used in the statistical, physical and theoretical analysis of language are applied to musical analysis.

871. Zeraschi, Helmut. *Drehorgel, Serinette und Barrel Organ.* 2 vols. Leipzig (phil.), 1961. Pp. 226, 132, illus., music.

872. Zimmerman, Franklin B. *A Survey of the Role of Music in Sonoran Uto-Aztecan Culture.* So. California, A.M., 1952. Pp. 228, music.
   A detailed analysis of music in an attempt to clarify styles in that culture area.

873. Zuniga-Tristan, Virginia. *Music in the Schools of Costa Rica.* Kentucky, M.A. (music ed.), 1943. Pp. 155.

INDEXES

Inquiries should be made to the department within each academic institution for which the dissertation or thesis was written. The following sources give detailed information on the institutions listed here.

American Universities and Colleges. Ed. by A. J. Brunbaugh. Washington, D.C., American Council on Education. Published every four years, 1928 + .

Index Generalis; Annuaire Général des Universités, . . . Paris, Editions Spes. Published periodically, 1919 + .

Minerva; Jahrbuch der gelehrten Welt. Strassburg, Trübner, and Berlin, de Gruyter. Published periodically, 1890 + .

Universities of the World Outside U. S. A. Ed. by M. M. Chambers. Washington, D.C., American Council on Education, 1950.

World of Learning. London, Europa Publications. Published periodically, 1947 + .

Index of Institutions

Aix, 551
(Université d'Aix-Marseille, Aix-en-Provence, France)
Amsterdam, 334
(Universiteit van Amsterdam, Amsterdam C., The Netherlands)
Arizona, 70, 130, 237, 281, 378, 842
(University of Arizona, Tucson, Arizona, U.S.A.)
Arizona S.C., 847
(Arizona State College, Flagstaff, Arizona, U.S.A.)

Basel, 68, 390
(Universität Basel, Petersplatz 1, Basel, Switzerland)
Baylor U., 363, 793
(Baylor University, Waco, Texas, U.S.A.)
Berlin, 57, 75, 222, 249, 322, 338, 351, 416, 434, 476, 581, 619, 638, 646,
667, 687, 733, 743, 789
(Universität Berlin. *Now* Humboldt-Universität zu Berlin. *See*
Berlin, H.U.)
Berlin, F.U., 132, 194, 433, 645, 697
(Freie Universität Berlin, Berlin-Dahlem, Boltzmahstrasse 4,
Germany. (West Sector))
Berlin, H.U., 347, 391, 650, 701, 761
(Humboldt-Universität zu Berlin, Berlin, W.8, Unter den Lin-
den 6, Germany. (East Sector))
Berlin, T.H., 534
(Technische Universität, Berlin-Charlottenburg 2, Harden-
bergstrasse 34, Germany. (West Sector))
Bern, 582, 617
(Universität Bern, Bern, Switzerland)
Bombay, 4
(University of Bombay, Bombay 1, India)
Bonn, 79, 85, 235, 412, 655, 755, 818, 833
(Rheinische Friedrich-Wilhelms-Universität, Bonn, Liebfrau-
enweg 3, Germany)
Boston U., 53, 128, 159, 196, 360, 388, 525, 600, 662, 704, 730, 757,
838, 858
(Boston University, 755 Commonwealth Avenue, Boston, Massa-
chusetts 02115, U.S.A.)
Breslau, 234
(Uniwersytet Wroclawski im Boleslawa Bieruta, Wroclaw Plac,
Uniwersytecki 1, Wroclaw (Breslau), Poland)
Brigham Young U., 293
(Brigham Young University, Provo, Utah, U.S.A.)

111

Brown U., 96, 176, 454, 554, 784
  (Brown University, Providence, Rhode Island, U.S.A.)
Bryn Mawr C., 67
  (Bryn Mawr College, Bryn Mawr, Pennsylvania, U.S.A.)

California, 268, 441, 477, 758, 816
  (*Now* California (Berkeley) *q.v.*)
California (Berkeley), 122, 339, 475, 491, 547, 548, 620
  (University of California, Berkeley, California 94704, U.S.A.)
California (Los Angeles), 43, 98, 100, 214, 246, 263, 308, 313, 396, 455,
  464, 480, 488, 506, 523, 557, 590, 711, 747, 769, 772
  (University of California, Los Angeles, 405 Hilgard Avenue,
  Los Angeles, California 90024, U.S.A.)
Cambridge (C.C.), 74
  (Christ's College, Cambridge University, Cambridge, England)
Catholic U., 400, 657, 664, 745, 780
  (The Catholic University of America, Fourth and Michigan
  Avenues, N.E., Washington, D.C. 20217, U.S.A.)
Central Wash. Coll. of Ed., 517
  (Central Washington College of Education. *Now* Central Wash-
  ington State College, Ellensburg, Washington, U.S.A.)
Chicago, 3, 22, 47, 48, 49, 162, 165, 204, 225, 272, 358, 371, 411, 457,
  538, 559, 739, 754, 774
  (University of Chicago, 5801 South Ellis Avenue, Chicago,
  Illinois 60637, U.S.A.)
Chicago Mus. Coll., 232
  (Chicago Musical College, 64 East Van Buren Street, Chicago,
  Illinois 60605, U.S.A.)
Cincinnati Conserv. of Music, 119
  (*Merged with* College of Music of Cincinnati *to become the*
  College-Conservatory of Music of Cincinnati, *q.v.*)
Claremont C., 26, 33, 392, 614
  (Claremont College. *Now* Claremont Graduate School and Uni-
  versity Center, Ninth Street and College Avenue, Claremont,
  California, U.S.A.)
Coll. of Music of Cincinnati, 144
  (College of Music of Cincinnati. *Merged with* Cincinnati Con-
  servatory of Music *to become the* College-Conservatory of Music
  of Cincinnati, *q.v.*)
College-Conserv. of Music of Cincinnati, 145, 449, 659, 702, 719, 763,
  785, 788, 800, 827, 836
  (College-Conservatory of Music of Cincinnati. *Affiliated with*
  University of Cincinnati, Highland Avenue and Oak Street,
  Cincinnati, Ohio 45221, U.S.A.)
Cologne, 279, 311, 397, 408, 689
  (Universität Köln, Köln (Cologne), Albertus-Magnus-Platz,
  Germany)

113

114

Idaho, 6, 837, 866
(University of Idaho, Moscow, Idaho, U.S.A.)
Illinois, 323, 381, 423, 855
(University of Illinois, Urbana, Illinois, U.S.A.)
Illinois Wesleyan U., 37, 399
(Illinois Wesleyan University, 210 East University Avenue, Bloomington, Illinois, U.S.A.)
Indiana U., 18, 27, 62, 73, 87, 105, 115, 164, 179, 189, 197, 224, 320, 355, 368, 385, 424, 482, 483, 503, 522, 549, 572, 574, 575, 603, 679, 696, 720, 727, 831, 835, 862, 867, 870
(Indiana University, Bloomington, Indiana 47401, U.S.A.)
Innsbruck, 418
(Leopold-Franzens Universität Innsbruck, Innsbruck, Innrain 52, Austria)
Iowa, 12, 25, 59, 66, 71, 113, 114, 183, 191, 229, 277, 324, 359, 370, 389, 485, 486, 492, 591, 595, 631, 635, 658, 723, 759, 768, 799, 825
(State University of Iowa, Iowa City, Iowa, U.S.A.)

Jena, 172, 285, 345, 712
(Friedrich-Schiller-Universität, Jena, Goetheallee 1, Germany)
Johns Hopkins U., 221
(Johns Hopkins University, Baltimore, Maryland 21218, U.S.A.)
Juilliard, 413
(Juilliard School of Music, 120 Claremont Avenue, New York, New York 10027, U.S.A.)

Kansas, 255, 336, 465, 599, 640, 673, 771, 804
(University of Kansas, Lawrence, Kansas, U.S.A.)
Kentucky, 489, 873
(University of Kentucky, Belknap Campus, Louisville, Kentucky 40208, U.S.A.)
Kiel, 186, 259, 562, 854
(Christian-Albrechts-Universität, Kiel, Neue Universität, Olshausenstrasse, Germany)
Königsberg, 505, 672
(*Now* Kaliningrad University (Königsberg), Kaliningrad, R.S. F.S.R. The university (Collegium Albertinium) was destroyed in World War II)

Laval U., 624, 681, 802, 869
(Laval University, Quebec 4, Quebec, Canada)
Leipzig, 16, 83, 104, 309, 341, 384, 419, 431, 612, 670, 686, 703, 773, 828, 871
(Karl-Marx-Universität, Leipzig C.1, Germany)
Liège, 856
(Université de Liège, Place du XX-Août, 7, Liège, Belgium)
Liverpool, 608
(University of Liverpool, Brownlow Hill, Liverpool 3, England)

Index of Subjects

Ability, aptitude and talent studies, 532, 599, 635, 669, 852; Alaska, 517; American Indians, 354, 669, 709, 834; Caucasians, 10, 61, 598, 669; Chinese, 364, 475; Filipinos, 287; Germans, 828; Hawaiians, 287, 364; Japanese, 364, 475, 669; Mexicans, 116, 598; mixed nationality and ethnic groups, 205, 245, 475, 517, 532, 852; Negroes, 10, 61, 365, 598; Portuguese, 287, 475; Spanish-Americans, 237, 475

Aboriginal music, Australia, 201, 285, 373, 374, 375, 561

Abraham, Priscilla Magdamo, field recordings collected in Philippines, 613

Accentuation, scriptural, 737

Accounts of music and dance in travelers' reports, 142, 147, 547, 835

Adventure songs, 559

Aegean Sea area, instruments, 5, 762

Aesthetics and music, 66, 164, 203, 235, 385, 431, 458, 538, 599, 856; *see also* Philosophy and music; Taste in music

Africa, Arab work songs, 228; Belgian Congo, 53, 82, 173, 311; Bulu, 404; Bushmen, 207; Cameroons, 404; Central, 279; dance, 63, 82, 387; Equatorial, 53, 82, 173, 247, 279, 311; East, 82, 329; Ibo, 193; instruments, 16, 53, 63, 82, 115, 193, 247, 276, 279, 311, 840; Kavirondo, 663; music, 63, 82, 173, 207, 247, 279, 329, 337, 338, 404, 663, 724; Nigeria, 338; Ruanda, 279; Ruanda-Urundi, 82, 311; South, 63, 115, 142, 207; Tanganyika, 82; Tiv, 338; Uganda, 82; Ungoni, 329; Venda, 63; West, 724

African Methodist Episcopal Church (U.S.), 177

African music, and European art music, 231, 546, 835; and jazz, 231, 292, 340, 360; bibliography, 780; rhythm, 337; survivals in Latin America, 18, 154, 232, 272, 360, 448, 531, 651, 822; survivals in U.S., 121, 231, 272, 292, 315, 340, 360, 395, 546, 579, 652; survivals in Western Hemisphere, 360

Agong music, Bagobo, 52

Alabama, folksongs, 98

Alaska, music and dance, 441, 490

Albania, funeral chants, 72

Albanian music and dance, in Yugoslavia, 330

Alps, folk music, 418; yodeling, 712

Altmark, folksongs, 761

American Indians, *see* Indians, American

Amish church music, 331

Anabaptist hymnody, 190

Analysis, music, African music, 63; Afro-Bahian songs, 531; American Indian music, 106, 130, 317, 400, 402, 479, 545, 574, 575, 732, 745, 800, 829, 872; Amish hymns and songs, 331; and language analysis techniques, 870; Armenian folksongs, 620; Assyrian folksongs, 578; Australian Aboriginal music, 373, 374, 561; Béla Bartók's music, 184, 775; Bulgarian folk music, 581, 757;

123

Carnatic *kriti*, 31; Chinese music, 788; Corsican laments, 433; Creole songs, 185, 675; East Indian music, 213, 625, 760; English folk music, 522, 729; European peasant songs, 611; folk music, U.S., 184, 185, 336, 348, 578, 601, 607; German and Scandinavian songs, 536; Hebrew and Jewish music, 708; Hungarian music, 208; Iberian music, 97; jazz, 631, 772, 808; lullabies, 239, 745; Mexican folksongs, 264, 556; Negro music, U.S., 159, 395, 662, 848; New Guinea music, 132; Okinawan classical songs, 442; *patet* in Javanese music, 334; Philippines tribal music, 613, 796; Polish folksongs, 262, 607; Protestant hymns, 747; Tlingit music, 510; Trinidad Negro music, 822; Turk music, 196; with electronic computers, 666, 831; *see also* Form; Harmony; Melody; Rhythm

Andalusian Gypsies, Deep Song, 633

Anglo-American ballad scholarship, 844

Antiquity, dance, 102, 149; instruments, 5, 221, 398, 730, 865; meter and rhythm, 252; music, 298, 431, 632; musicians' associations, 226; songs, 457; *see also* China; Greece; Rome

Antwerp, songbook, 325

Appalachians, folksongs, 336

Aptitude, music, constructs of, 635; *see also* Ability, aptitude and talent

Arabian music, 564; in B. Bartók's works, 184; in Egypt, 57; influence on Spanish music, 471, 657; influence on troubadours, 1; religious music, 227; work songs, 228

Archaeology and music, 33, 518

Argentina, Indian music, 748

Aristotle and music, 417, 650, 789

Armenia, folk music, 174; folksongs, 26, 620; instruments, 174

Armenians in U.S., folksongs, 601

Arnhem Land, Aboriginal music, 373, 374

Art music,

composers utilizing folk or ethnic materials: Armenian, 174; B. Bartók, 184, 611, 775; L. van Beethoven, 346; J. Brahms, 178, 552; Brazilian, 18; B. Brecht, 497; C. Chavez, 368, 769; A. Copland, 726; English, 437; French, 657; G. Gershwin, 630, 770; L. M. Gottschalk, 185; E. Grieg, 258, 359; H. Isaac, 670; C. Ives, 468; Mexican, 35, 368, 543, 769; Negro, 251; Norwegian, 749; K. Othmayr, 670; Russian, 657, 781; L. Senfl, 670; B. F. Smetanas, 697; I. Stravinsky, 113; U.S., 73, 289, 614, 746, 792; R. Vaughan Williams, 56, 522, 608

contributions of: African Negro, 231, 546, 835; American Indian, 6, 12, 35, 73, 135, 289, 468, 827, 835; exotic cultures, 835; English folk music, 729; folklore, 701; jazz, 43, 73, 468, 630, 726, 770; Negro, U.S., 113, 289, 358, 405, 546, 790, 792; Polish dance music, 443; Welsh in U.S., 614

in epoch of imperialism, 701; India, 213, 394, 505; influence of World War I on, 797; Japan, 458; Java, 334; Persian, 214, 397, 503; physiological effects of, 558; Turkey, 197; *see also* Opera

Asia, instruments, 398, 865; peasant songs, 611; Arab work songs, 228

Asia Minor, folksongs, 620

Associations, musicians', 467; in antiquity, 226; in Germany, 462, 560, 685, 779

Assyria, instruments, 221, 730

Assyrians in U.S., folksongs and instruments, 578
Attitudes, of rural children regarding music, 349; of Soviet culture toward
    music, 215; of Spanish-Americans as expressed in *coplas,* 502;
    of U.S. composers, 571
Aulos, 343
Australia, Aboriginal music, 201, 285, 373, 374, 561; Aboriginal instru-
    ments, 375
Austria, folk music, 283, 418; military bands, 593
Austrians in U.S., music aptitude, 205

Babylonian music, 737
Baden, folksongs, 428
Baer, Abraham, *Bā'al Tefillah,* 690
Bagobo, ceremonial music, 52
Bahian cult music, 531, 651
Bali, *gamelan anklung,* 590
Ballads, Anglo-American scholarship, 844; bibliography, 444, 493, 540;
    British, 32, 478, 540, 591, 704; Canada, 167, 321, 500, 849;
    catalogs and collections, 540; Christian elements in, 833; com-
    munal composition of, 152; Czech, 152; Denmark, 535; English,
    79, 80, 99, 100, 265, 339, 438, 478, 500, 535, 706, 813, 833;
    "The Farmer's Curst Wife," 99; Finnish, 152; "Frankie and Al-
    bert," 105; German, 188, 497; "Get Up and Bar the Door," 99;
    Indiana, 87, 572; Iowa, 71, 768; Kentucky, 71; love, 596; mel-
    ody and rhythm, 23, 79; Mississippi, 344; Negro, 444; North
    American, 137, 833; Norwegian, 198; "Our Goodman," 99;
    Ozark, 348; Russian, 152; Scottish, 79, 99, 100, 339, 493, 500,
    535, 596, 706, 833; social criticism in, 706; Spanish, 501; tune
    variants, 339; U.S., 23, 30, 32, 46, 65, 71, 76, 78, 87, 99, 100,
    105, 141, 151, 265, 321, 332, 339, 344, 348, 444, 549, 572, 591,
    768, 844; "The Wife Wrapt in Wether's Skin," 99; *see also*
    Child Ballads
Baltic, peasant songs, 611
Bands, military, 593, 628; Mormon, 628; sociological aspects of, 469;
    see also Dance bands
Baptist church, hymnody, 868
"Barbara Allen," versions of, 549
Baroque, music and medicine in, 384
Bartók, Béla, 184, 611, 775
Bavaria, folksongs, 674
Bawdy songs, 46
Bear ceremonials, Northern Hemisphere, 288
Bear Dance, Ute, 293
Beethoven, Ludwig van, 346
Belgian Congo, dance, 82; instruments, 53, 82, 311; music, 82, 173
Belgium, folksongs, 93, 325
Berlin Phonogrammarchiv, 132
Bible, changing emphasis of music in, 830
Bibliographies, African music, 780; ballads, 444, 493, 540; dance, 160,
    306; folk music, 156, 306; hymnbooks, 466, 864; jazz, 340;
    Minnesota music, 254; Negro music, 251; North American In-
    dian music, 306, 320; songbooks, 58; tune books, 89, 206, 466;
    versions of "Barbara Allen," 549; *see also* Catalogs

Bismarck Archipelago, music, 345
"Black is the Color of My True Love's Hair," 746
Bluegrass, 727
Blues, 121, 474, 710, 811
Boeckh, August (1785-1876), and Greek music, 447
Bolivia, Indian music, 748
Borobudur, instruments, 569
Bow, musical, in South Africa, 115
Brahms, Johannes, 178, 552
Brandenburg, military music, 646
Brazil, composers' use of indigenous music, 18; folk, Indian and Portu-
    guese music, 18, 748; Negro music, 18, 531, 651
Brecht, Bertolt, 497
Brethren of Christ, function of music among, 677
British in U.S., ballads and music, 542, 591; music ability and aptitude,
    205, 245
Bücher, Karl, *Arbeit und Rhythmus* (1896), 104
Bugaku, 857
Bulgaria, Byzantine music, 594; Christmas carols, 667; dance, 736, 757;
    epic songs, 422, 606; folk music, 623, 736, 757; folksongs, 34,
    83, 581, 582, 623; funeral chants, 72; instruments, 736, 757;
    popular songs, 184
Bulu songs, from Cameroons, 404
Burma, music, 644
Bushman music, 207
Byzantine music, 594, 805; influence on Spanish music, 657

Cable, George Washington, and jazz, 725
Cades Cove, Tennessee, heritage and folk music of, 242
California, dance, 238, 392, 455, 464, 585; folk music, 539, 555; German-
    American singing societies, 182; mission music, 335
California, University of (Berkeley), collection of recordings, 64
Calumet Dance, 218
Calypso songs, Virgin Islands, 439
Cameroons, Bulu songs, 404
Camp meetings, hymns of, 717
Campaign songs, U.S., 17
Canada, ballads, 167, 321, 500, 849; folksongs, 167, 355, 499, 500, 869;
    French in, 167, 520, 624, 665, 738, 802, 869; Maritime Prov-
    inces, 355; Miramichi Valley, 849; Nova Scotia, 500
Cantilation, scriptural, 737
Caribbean, calypso, 439; European cultural elements in music and dance,
    448; *see also* Latin America
Carnatic music, study of *tala* in, 586
Carols, 388; Bulgaria, 667; Christmas, 592, 667; English, folk, 126; Latin
    America, 592; pre-Reformation, 525
Catalogs, British ballads, 540; Chinese songs, 45; Civil War songs, 96;
    Maori song collections, 496; songsters, U.S., 176, 454, 784
Caucasians, music ability, 10, 61, 598, 669
Central America, 713; school music, 610, 873; *see also* Latin America

126

Ceremonial music, American Indians, 70, 122, 189, 281, 293, 479, 723, 800, 806, 829, 847, 853, 866; Bagobo, 52; Bear, 288; China, 47; Eskimo, 441; Green Corn, 853; Holy Land Christians, 227; Japan, 767; Northern Hemisphere, 288; Oceania, 223; *see also* Ritual music

Ceremonies, American Indians, 122, 479, 829; Holy Land Christians, 227

Chansons, French-Canadian, 802, 869; Louisiana, 681

Chanteys, Canada, 167, 321; texts, 117; U.S., 315, 321, 444, 559, 702

Chants, African, 232; Bagobo, 52; funeral, 72; Graeco-Slavonic, 326; Hebrew, 269; Hopi Indians, 62; Maori, 496; Mozarabic, 11; Puerto Rico, 232; Russian Orthodox church, 326; Slavonic, 805

Character notes, 466

Chavez, Carlos, 368, 769

Cheremis folksongs, 208

Cherokee Outlet, folk music, 460

Chiapas, folk music, 264

Chicago, dance musicians, 49; Negro songs in church ritual, 162

Child Ballads, 32, 65, 87, 137, 141, 265, 549

Children, attitude regarding music, 349; melodic sensitivity, 10; melodies composed by, 765

    music ability, aptitude and talent:
        American Indian, 669, 834; Caucasian, 10, 598, 669; Chinese, 475; Filipino, 287; Hawaiian, 287; Japanese, 669; Mexican, 116, 598; mixed nationality and racial groups, 245, 475; Negro, 10, 598; Portuguese, 287, 475

Children's music, Africa, 663; change in, 259; Japan, 523

Children's songs, 765; Franconia, 69; Germany, 69, 429, 562; Latin America, 801; U.S., 591; Venda, 63

China, ancient music, 47, 48, 123, 527, 661; church music, 216; classic opera, 818; instruments, 123, 730, 782, 788; lü in, 661; missionary schools, 664; music history, 222, 782, 788; music sources, 615; orchestras, 341; polyphonic treatment of tunes, 838; songs, 45; Sung Dynasty, 45, 615; T'ang Dynasty, 430; tonal systems, 430; *see also* Far East

Chinese, influence on Japanese music, 295; music aptitude and talent, 364, 475

Chinese culture, influence of music on, 527; music in, 839

Chinese music, in France, 776; in Western art music, 835; relationships with Okinawan classical songs, 442; theoretical aspects of, 860

Christian elements, in folk ballads, 833; in Hebrew music, 708

Christian Judgment Service music, 815

Church music, African Methodist Episcopal, 177; Amish, 331; Anabaptist, 190; Armenia, 174; Baptist, 868; Brethren of Christ, 677; Chinese, 216; Christian Judgment Service, 815; Coptic, 55; German, 108; Jewish, 187, 269, 507, 690, 708, 737; Lutheran, 722, 855; Mennonite, 864; Methodist Episcopal, 323; Moravian, 389, 482, 483; Mormon, 191, 445, 480, 628, 720, 826; Negro, 162, 177, 721; Presbyterian, 515; Protestant, 747, 859; Russian Orthodox, 326; *see also* Hymns and hymnody; Psalms and psalmody; Religious music

Civil War, U.S., songs, 96, 858

Collections, American Indian recordings, 64, 385; American poetry, 96; British ballads, 540; Canadian folksongs, 869; East Indian recordings, 217; English ballad refrains, 80; Italian folksongs, 256; Malekulan recordings, 134; Maori music, 496; Negro folksong texts, 477; Negro spirituals, 533; New Guinea recordings, 132; U.S. folksongs, 363, 793; U.S. popular songs, 328
Colleges and universities, folk dance in, 296; Negro music in, 436, 604; student dance bands in, 175, 366
Communism and music, 215
Community and folksong, 88
Composers, and folklore, 701; and nationalism, 35, 56, 73, 468, 543, 781; and political ideologies, 202, 215, 701; as themes for literary works, 655, 693, 735; Brazil, 18; English virginal, 437; folksong, 273; India, 213, 394; Japanese, 458; Mexico, 35; National Socialist Germany, 202; Negro, 251; Norwegian, 749; popular music, 67, 212, 783; Russia, 781; Soviet Union, 202; U.S., 73, 202, 212, 251, 468, 571, 746, 783, 792, 827; *see also* Art music
Composition, communal, 152; contemporary Japan, 458; India, 213
Computer, electronic, and music analysis, 666, 831; and music transcription, 589
Conchero dancers, Mexico, 508
Congo, *see* Belgian Congo
Copland, Aaron, 726
Coplas, Spanish-American, 502
Coptic church music, 55
Corn Dance, North American Indian, 357, 728
Correctional institutions, use of music in, 465; *see also* Reformatories
Corsica, laments, 433
Costa Rica, school music, 873
Court music, Japan, 301
Cowboy songs and ballads, 73, 315, 460, 580, 591, 702
Creole songs and folk music, U.S., 121, 185, 579, 675
Croatia, folksongs, 419
Cuba, music, 36, 112, 154; instruments and dance, 36
Czechoslovakia, folk music, 697; folksongs, 799
Czechoslovakians, ballads, 152; dance, 464, 809; folk music, 820; music aptitude, 205; in U.S., 205, 464, 809, 820

Dance, Africa, 63, 82, 387; ancient Egypt, 102; ancient Greece, 526, 544, 626; and visual arts and music, 734; Armenia, 174; Bear Dance, 288, 293; bibliography of, 160, 306; Bulgaria, 736, 757; California, 238, 392, 455, 464, 585; Caribbean, 448; classic, Far East, 812; classic, Greek, 526; Colonial America, 25; Corn Dance, 357, 728; Cuba, 36; Czech, 464, 809; Deer Dance, 842; Eagle Dance, 218; economic influences on, 40; English, 126; Eskimo, 490; ethnologic approach, 25; European, 324; Far East, 812; folk, 4, 29, 42, 69, 103, 126, 146, 170, 174, 238, 290, 296, 305, 314, 324, 370, 392, 410, 448, 461, 627, 641, 647, 658, 679, 707; Franconia, 29, 69; genetic phases of, 161; Germany, 29, 69, 314, 410, 528, 641; Ghost Dance, 169, 514, 715; Greek, 526; Green Corn Dance, 660, 853; Hawaiian Islands, 147; Himalayan, 679; Hungarian, 464, 637; Iberian, 97; in education, 8,

103, 175, 369, 370, 595, 707, 764, 809, 846; India, 4, 679; Irish, 387; *jarabe tapatio,* 157; *jota aragonesa,* 97; Kumanche Dance, 124; Mallorca, 42; mask in, 44; Medicine Dance, 634; Melanesia, 689; mentioned in travelers' reports, 147, 835; Mexican, 369, 392, 455, 627; Mexico, 7, 157, 284, 361, 367, 508, 577, 627; modern, 386, 825; Negro, 63, 82, 387; New Guinea, 689; New Mexico, 8, 509; New York City, 707; North America, 306; Northern Hemisphere, 288; notation, 387, 711; Oriental, 386, 825; origins and development, 40, 248, 290, 461, 648; Philippine Islands, 446, 647; play-party, 77; Polish, 435, 443; Pomerania, 410; pre-classic forms, 131; primitive motivations of, 181; Provençale, 551; Puget Sound, 841; religious, 40, 120, 149; rhythm, 485, 734; ritual, 508, 634, 812; Russian, 753; sacred, 812; Scottish, 387; social, 192, 528; social influences on, 4, 40; Society Islands, 147; Spanish, 97, 248; Spanish-American, 8, 25, 392, 509; Sun Dance, 695, 741, 766, 806; Swedish, 464, 764; teaching of, 370; terminology, 170; U.S., 8, 25, 73, 103, 170, 238, 296, 387, 392, 455, 464, 509, 585, 658, 707, 734, 764, 846; Yugoslavia, 330; *see also* Indians, American, dance

Dance and religion, 120, 149, 281, 723
Dance bands, German, 425; U.S. schools, 175, 366
Dance musicians in Chicago, 49
Dance of Death, in folksong, 754
Danish, folksongs, 376, 535; music aptitude, 205
Dastgah, 214, 397, 503
Davenport, Iowa, music history of, 59
Death Song, American Indian, 371
Deep Song, Andalusian Gypsies, 633
Deer Dance, 842
Democracy and music, 426
Denmark, ballads, 535; folksongs, 376
Densmore, Frances, 189
Detroit, Polish folksongs, 607
Dicey Catalog of Old Ballads (Bodleian), 540
Didjeridu, Australia, 375
Discographies, folk music and folksong, 103, 306, 843; jazz, 340; *see also* Recordings
Drama and music, 6, 111, 135, 168, 409, 432, 459, 497, 527, 563, 565, 587, 628, 699, 719, 803, 807, 813, 835, 867
Drums, 244; Africa, 840; Eskimo, 490; India, 394
Dutch, music aptitude, 205

Eagle Dance, 218
East Africa, dance, 82; instruments, 82; music, 82, 330
Eclipse rituals, North American Indians, 13
Economic influences, on origin of dance, 40
Economic problems, of musicians, 519
Economics and music, 67
Ecuador, Indian music, 748
Education and dance, 8, 103, 296, 369, 370, 707, 764, 809, 846

Education and music, 8, 14, 37, 60, 81, 89, 103, 118, 129, 167, 175, 180,
    183, 198, 202, 204, 271, 302, 307, 308, 316, 318, 332, 350, 366,
    369, 376, 378, 391, 393, 411, 414, 436, 445, 452, 466, 484, 487,
    512, 555, 566, 573, 595, 604, 610, 628, 629, 643, 650, 654, 671,
    677, 684, 691, 707, 719, 720, 738, 740, 744, 759, 764, 771, 777,
    778, 795, 798, 799, 804, 829, 845, 847, 873
Egerland, folksongs, 236
Egypt, ancient, dance, 102; instruments, 221; songs, 457
Egypt, Arabic music, 57; Coptic church music, 55
Egyptian music, in France, 678
El Salvador, school music, 610
Electronic computers, use in music analysis and transcription, 589, 666,
    831
Elementary schools, American Indian music, 233, 308, 318; folksongs,
    629; music education, 691; use of folk materials in, 103, 233,
    350, 414, 707; see also Schools
Emerson, Ralph Waldo, and folksong, 65
Emotion in music, 538
Engel, Grace L., music analysis of Polish folksongs of Detroit, 607
England, ballads, 79, 80, 265, 339, 438, 478, 706, 813; folk carols and
    dance, 126; folk music, 263, 729; folklore, 263; folksongs, 56,
    333, 339, 414, 437, 478, 522, 608; hymns and hymnody, 600,
    868; music hall songs, 807; popular songs, 813; see also Great
    Britain
English ballads and folksongs, in Denmark, 535; in North America, 99,
    100, 141, 265, 336, 339, 500, 833; see also British
Epic songs, Bulgaria, 422, 606
Equatorial Africa, dance, instruments and music, 82, 247
Eskimo, ceremonials, 441; dance, 490; drums, 490; music, 211; songs,
    167, 490, 510
Estonia, folksongs, 266; musical life in, 24
Ethics, and ancient Greek music, 417
Ethiopia, Coptic church music, 55
Ethnomusicological archives, Berlin, 132; California, University of (Berke-
    ley), 64; Indiana University, 385; Layard Collection, 134;
    Vienna, Phonogramm-Archiv, 217
Ethos, in Greek music, 2, 15, 659
Europe, exotic music in drama, 835; folk music teaching under UNESCO,
    654; medieval music instruments, 521, 863
European culture elements, in American Indian music, 130; in Caribbean
    music and dance, 448; in Illinois folksongs, 601; in Minnesota
    music, 254; in Negro music of U.S., 652; survivals in Iowa
    festivals, 512
Europeans, folk dances and singing games, 324; music aptitude in school
    children, 475
Exotic music, form, 362; in European drama, 835

Far East, sacred, classic, court and ritual dance, 812
"Farmer's Curst Wife," 99
Festivals, dance, 577; European survivals in U.S., 464, 512; folk, 512;
    harvest, 357; Iowa, 512; Los Angeles, 464; Mexico, 577; Ute
    Indian, 293

Fiddle tunes, North Carolina, 54
Field work, in Maori music, 496; manuals, 261
Filipino children, music talent, 287
Finnish, ballads, 152; folk music and songs in U.S., 452, 601
Florida, folk music, 820; folksongs, 107, 501, 553
Folk dance, *see* Dance, folk
Folk hero, in U.S. folksong texts, 541
Folk instruments, 377, 865, 871
Folk music, 529; American Indian, 145, 189, 289, 542, 643; Arabian, 184;
    Armenia, 174; Austria, 283, 418; Bavaria, 674; bibliography,
    156, 306; bluegrass, 727; Brazil, 18; Bulgaria, 623, 736, 757;
    California, 539, 555; Caribbean, 448; Creole, 185; Czech, 697,
    820; discography, 103, 843; early settlers in U.S., 580; England,
    263, 729; Eskimo, 211, 490; fiddle tunes, 54; field work in, 261,
    496; Finnish, 452; Florida, 820; for hunting, 773; France, 657;
    French, 69, 542, 624, 665; German, 59, 671; Germany, 314,
    674, 756; Greek, 350; Holy Land Christians, 227; Hungary,
    184, 208, 236; in education, 8, 60, 81, 89, 103, 118, 129, 204,
    233, 307, 316, 350, 414, 452, 555, 573, 604, 643, 654, 671, 720,
    764, 778, 795, 845; in opera, 263, 396, 697, 700; India, 679;
    instrumental, 54, 114, 283, 727; Jamaica, 270; Jewish, 230;
    Kentucky, 114, 125; Latin America, 18, 185, 232, 270, 448;
    Louisiana, 121, 185, 542, 579; melodies, 22, 249; Mexico, 264,
    367, 543, 556; Monongahela Valley, 78; Negro, 18, 113, 121,
    145, 251, 289, 580, 662; Netherlands, 101; New Mexico, 8;
    North Carolina, 54; Norway, 258, 359, 749; Persian, 503;
    Polynesia, 498; Portuguese, 18, 539; Prussia, 672; Puerto Rico,
    232; Rumania, 184; scales, 729; Serbo-Croatian, 184, 240;
    Shakers, 143; Slovakia, 184; Slovenia, 129; Spanish, 8, 204, 232;
    Swedish, 764; Tennessee, 242; Texas, 850; Turkish, 184;
    Ukrainia, 184; U.S., 8, 54, 59, 73, 78, 103, 114, 121, 125, 129,
    143, 145, 150, 156, 185, 225, 242, 251, 262, 289, 306, 307,
    315, 350, 396, 414, 452, 468, 474, 512, 539, 541, 542, 555,
    579, 580, 614, 624, 654, 662, 702, 727, 764, 820, 823, 850
Folklore and music, 701; American Indian, 847; England, 263; Great
    Britain, 704; North America, 306, 321; U.S., 261, 396, 680, 682
Folksinger, popular image of, 603
Folksongs, 529, 534, 597; adventure, 559; aesthetics of, 235; Alabama,
    98; Altmark, 761; Appalachians, 336; Arab, 228; Armenia, 26,
    620; Armenian, 601; Asia Minor, 620; Assyrian, 578; Baden,
    428; Bavaria, 674; bawdy, 46; Belgium, 93, 325; bibliography,
    306; "Black is the Color of My True Love's Hair," 746; British,
    591; Bulgaria, 34, 83, 581, 582, 623; calypso, 439; Canada, 167,
    355, 499, 500, 869; carols, 126, 388, 592, 667; chansons, 681,
    802, 869; chanteys, 46, 117, 167, 315, 321, 444, 559, 702;
    Cheremis, 208; collections, 256, 363, 793, 869; community, 88;
    composers of, 273; computer analysis of, 831; cowboy, 73, 315,
    460, 580, 591, 702; Creole, 121, 185, 579, 675; critical study of,
    844; Croatia, 419; Czech, 799; Dance of Death in, 754; Denmark, 376; Detroit, 607; discography, 306, 843; early settlers
    in U.S., 460; England, 56, 333, 339, 414, 437, 478, 522, 608;
    English, 141, 336, 500; Eskimo, 167, 490; Estonia, 266; farmer,

131

273; Finnish, 452, 601; Florida, 107, 501, 553; form, 253; France, 93, 188, 336, 414, 504, 742; Franconia, 69; French, 680, 681; French-Canadian, 167, 520, 802, 869; frontier, 559; German, 59, 182, 266, 382, 552, 671, 777; Germany, 3, 69, 93, 104, 235, 253, 303, 309, 333, 336, 347, 352, 382, 406, 408, 410, 412, 414, 415, 423, 428, 476, 524, 536, 552, 576, 584, 619, 622, 668, 670, 683, 684, 692, 694, 698, 716, 742, 755, 761, 777, 814, 828, 854; Greece, 195, 623; harmony in, 291, 757; Himalayan, 679; Hinsbeck, 412; historical study of, 844; hobo, 315; Holland, 93; Hungary, 208, 236; Iberian, 97, 657; Illinois, 601; in education, 8, 14, 37, 103, 167, 183, 198, 302, 332, 376, 414, 487, 595, 629, 707, 771, 777, 798, 799; in youth movement, 282; India, 679; Indiana, 87, 572; Iowa, 71, 768; Irish, 150, 583; Istra, 718; Italian, 256; Japanese, 21; Jewish, 601; Kansas, 862; Kentucky, 702; Korea, 14, 401; labor, 220, 273; Latin-America, 414; Latvia and Lithuania, 382; Lorraine, 188, 742; Louisiana, 591, 624, 680, 787; love, 98; lullabies, 239, 318, 745; lumberjack, 46, 321, 444, 702; Maine, 46, 355; Mallorca, 42; manhood, 559; Maritime Provinces, 355; melodies of, 22, 34, 249, 291, 336, 352, 623, 672, 854; meter, 83, 581; Mexican, 595; Middle Ages, 755; migrant worker, 273; miner, 273, 309, 450; Mississippi, 315, 344; Missouri, 486, 591; modality in, 522; Mormons, 628, 720; Negro, U.S., 65, 121, 159, 225, 255, 273, 315, 358, 395, 405, 444, 474, 477, 546, 559, 579, 580, 675, 702, 787, 792, 793, 811, 837, 848; New Mexico, 771; North America, 306; Norwegian, 183, 198; Oberhessen, 352; occupational, 121; of Forty-Niners, 268; Ohio River songs, 836; Oklahoma, 591; Olympic Peninsula, 413; outlaws and criminals, 559; Ozark, 348; parodies, 98; Pennsylvania, 450; Philippine Islands, 27, 487; play-party, 77, 163, 591; Polish, 262, 435, 607; Pomerania, 410; prairie, 468; protest, 273; Prussia, 672; Puget Sound, 413; Pyrenees, 383; quodlibet as source of, 612; railroad, 702; recordings of, 306, 450, 843; religious, 395, 716; revival movements, 333, 603; Rhone, 504; rhythm in, 83, 253, 262, 581, 686, 757; river, 559, 836; Rumania, 199, 656; Russia, 414, 700, 781; sacred, 26; satirical, 98, 355, 565; Scandinavian, 302, 536; sentimental, 98; Serbian, 421; Serbo-Croatian, 240; Slovenia, 601; social, 291, 617; social commentary, 98; Spanish-American, 502, 509, 771; strophic development in, 619; Sturm und Drang period, 406; Swabia, 415, 683; Swedish, 573, 601; Texas, 107, 141, 591; textile workers, 273; Thrace, 623; Thuringia, 692; tonality in, 21, 623; Turkish, 179; U.S., 8, 17, 37, 46, 65, 77, 87, 96, 98, 99, 100, 103, 107, 121, 141, 150, 151, 163, 167, 183, 198, 225, 255, 262, 267, 268, 273, 302, 306, 315, 319, 321, 332, 336, 339, 344, 348, 355, 358, 363, 414, 450, 468, 477, 486, 492, 501, 509, 541, 553, 559, 572, 578, 579, 580, 591, 595, 601, 603, 607, 614, 628, 629, 639, 675, 680, 681, 707, 720, 726, 746, 768, 771, 777, 787, 792, 793, 811, 831,836, 837, 843, 848, 862; variants and variations in, 78, 437, 499, 639, 851; Virginia, 141; war, 96, 315, 449, 559, 576, 698, 858; Washington, 413; Welsh, 614; West Virginia, 141, 151, 639; work, 104, 228, 474, 694

Form, exotic music, 362; German folksongs, 253; music of India, 286; music of nonliterate peoples, 310; *see also* Analysis

Forty-Niners, songs of, 268

France, Chinese music in, 776; composers, 657; Egyptian music in, 678; folksongs, 93, 188, 336, 414, 504, 742; popular songs, 94; social status of musicians, 588

Franconia, folksongs and children's songs, 69; folk dance, 29, 69

"Frankie and Albert," 105

French, Equatorial Africa, 82; in North America, 738; music aptitude, 205

French folk music and songs, in Germany, 69; in Canada, 167, 520, 624, 665, 802, 869; in Louisiana, 542, 624, 680, 681

Friedrich, Grafen, folksongs of, 325

Frontier songs, 559

Function of music, 495; and aesthetics, 856; Brethren of Christ, 677; Chinese culture, 839; Deep Song of Andalusian Gypsies, 633; Islamic culture, 200; of Bertolt Brecht, 497; *see also* Role of music

Funeral chants, Rumania and Serbia, 72

Gagaku, 246

Gamelan anklung, Bali, 590

Geiger, Bernhard, translator of East Indian song texts, 217

Georgia, public school music among Negroes, 81

Germans, music ability and aptitude, 205, 245, 828; music of, in other countries, 59, 108, 182, 205, 245, 266, 382, 552, 671, 777

Germany, ballads, 188, 497; change in musical style, 638; children's songs, 69, 429, 562; composer and political ideology in, 202; dance bands, 425; folk dance, 29, 69, 314, 410, 528, 641; folk music, 314, 674; folksongs, 3, 69, 93, 104, 235, 253, 303, 309, 333, 336, 347, 352, 382, 406, 408, 410, 412, 414, 415, 428, 476, 524, 536, 552, 576, 584, 619, 622, 668, 670, 683, 684, 692, 694, 698, 716, 742, 755, 761, 777, 814, 828, 854; influence of phonograph records and radio on music instrument industry, 84; instruments, 794; Jewish music in, 451, 690; *kiltlied,* 668; *loblied,* 423; music and youth, 756; music in literature of, 655, 693; musicians, 693, 817; musicians' associations, 462, 560, 685, 779; vaudeville in, 459

Gershwin, George, 630, 770

"Get Up and Bar the Door," 99

Ghost Dance, 169, 514

Ghost Dance Religion, 715

Glazer, Joe, 273

Glossary, of musical terms used by Plato, 15

Gorman, Larry, 355

Gospel songs, 403, 494; Caucasian, 260; in southern Presbyterianism, 515; influence on Christian hymnody, 609; influence on Negro church, 721; Negro, 474, 652

Gottschalk, Louis Moreau, 185

Graeco-Slavonic chant, 326

Great Britain, ballad scholarship, 844; folklore, 704; songs and ballads, 32, 478, 540, 704

Greece, ancient, music, 527; and aesthetics, 164; and dance, 526, 544, 626; and education, 484, 566, 740; and ethics, 417; and ethos, 2, 15, 659; and philosophy, 123; choral songs, 111; harmony, 447; history, 275, 763; in life and thought, 74, 719; instruments, 343, 440, 730; modes, 86; social aspects, 616; therapy, 68; *see also* Antiquity; Aristotle; Plato
Greece, folksongs, 195, 623
Greek-Americans, music aptitude, 205; folk music, 350
Green Corn Dance, 660, 853
Gregorian chant, 55
Grieg, Edvard H., 258, 359
Gusle, Yugoslavia, 861
Guthrie, Woodie, 273
Gypsy music, 119; Hungary, 38; Spain, 633, 657

Haiti, African music survivals in, 272
Hambach, Kr. Saargemünd, 742
Hamburg, musicians' associations, 462
Hanoverian Succession, songs and ballads loyal to, 478
Harmonic sensitivity, Negro and Caucasian children, 10
Harmony, ancient Greek music, 447; Bulgarian folk music, 757; social songs, 291; *see also* Analysis
Harp, ancient Orient to medieval Europe, 863
Harpers' songs, 457
Harris Collection of American Poetry and Plays (Brown University), 96
Hawaiian Islands, dance, 147; music, 744, 778, 798
Hawaiians, music talent, 287, 364
Hearn, Lafcadio, 725
Heathens, ancient, music, 632
Hebrew music, 269, 481, 708; instruments, 221, 708, 730; *see also* Israel; Jewish music; Semitic music
Hellenic music, 15
Herder, Johann G., 65
Hiawatha (tone poem), 135
Hibeli Musical Papyrus, 15
High schools, *see* Secondary schools
Himalayan, dance, folksongs, and instruments, 679
Hindustani music, 394
Hinsbeck, folksongs, 412
Hispanic elements, in Mexican music, 35
History and music, 32, 763, 844
Hobo songs, 315
Holland, folksongs, 93; *see also* Netherlands
Hollers, 121
Holy Land Christians, folk music, 227
Hungarians in U.S., dance, 464; music aptitude, 205
Hungary, dance, 637; folk music, 184, 208, 236; instruments, 38; religious music, 38
Hunting, music for, 773
Hymn books, bibliography, 466, 864
Hymns and hymnody, 403, 515; Armenia, 26; camp-meeting tradition, 717; Denmark, 376; England, 600; Germany, 190, 451; in

compositions of Charles Ives, 468; Lutheran, 855; Mexico, 508; Mozarabic, 11; Protestant, 747; Syria, 172; U.S., 109, 177, 323, 331, 468, 515, 717, 722, 826, 864; Wesleyan, 323, 550; *see also* Church music

Iberia, folksongs, 97, 657
Ibo, instruments, 193
Iconography, music instruments, in Spanish Romanesque, 821; at Borobu-
 dur, 569
Illinois, folksongs, 601
Improvisation, 391; jazz, 140; to 1600, 219
Indian (East) music, 353, 394; and dance, 4, 679; art, 213, 394, 505;
 folksongs, 679; form, 286; in *Natya Sastra*, 85; instruments, 213,
 394, 679; *kriti*, 31; notation, 213; philosophic background, 568;
 raga, 213, 394, 516, 625; recorded collection of, 217; *tabla*, 760;
 tala, 213, 394, 586; Vedic and classic, 217
Indiana, ballads and songs, 87, 572
Indiana University, Archives of Traditional Music, 385
Indians, American
 dance, 13, 25, 106, 144, 411, 567, 705, 766, 827; bibliography, 306;
  Calumet Dance, 218; Corn Dance, 357, 728; Deer Dance, 842;
  Green Corn Dance, 660, 853; Ghost Dance, 169, 514, 715;
  Kumanche Dance, 124; Medicine Dance, 634; Sun Dance, 741,
  806; tribes: Algonkian, 853; Algonquin, 846; Arapaho, 715;
  Arizona, 70; Aztec, 284, 367; Blackfoot, 846; California, 139;
  Caribbean, 448; Cherokee, 853; Cheyenne, 385, 715; Chontal,
  7; City Dionysia, 695; Conchero, 508; Cora, 7; Creek, 357, 853;
  Crow, 277, 806; Eastern Woodlands, 853; Fort Hall, 695; Hopi,
  847; Huastec, 7; Huave, 7; Huichol, 7; Iroquois, 853; Jemez,
  728; Kiowa, 241; Kwakiutl, 50; Lacandon, 7; Makah, 846;
  Maya, 7, 284; Mayo, 7; Menomini, 634; Mexico, 7, 361, 367;
  Moqui, 50; Nahatl, 7; Oglala, 715; Ojibwa, 634; Otomi, 7;
  Paiute, 514; Papago, 281, 723; Pima, 281, 317, 723; Plains, 741;
  Pueblo, 95, 317, 660, 728, 846; Puget Sound, 841; Santo Do-
  mingo, 728; Seneca, 218, 732; Seri, 7; Shoshone, 695, 806; Sia,
  728; Siouan, southeastern, 853; Sioux, 846; Tairona, 518; Taos
  Pueblo, 95; Tarahumara, 7; Tarasco, 7; Tojolabales, 7; Totonac,
  7; Tzeltal, 7; Tzotzil, 7; Ute, 293, 372; Winnebago, 634; Yaqui,
  7, 70, 842; Zapotec, 7; Zuni, 124
 instruments, tribes: Arapaho, 574; California, 122, 472; Cheyenne,
  385; Chontal, 7; Cora, 7; Huastec, 7; Huave, 7; Huichol, 7;
  Inca, 110; Lacandon, 7; Maya, 7; Mayo, 7; Mexico, 7; Nahatl,
  7; Otomi, 7; Seneca, 732; Seri, 7; South America, 356; Tairona,
  518; Tarahumara, 7; Tarasco, 7; Tojolabales, 7; Totonac, 7;
  Tzeltal, 7; Tzotzil, 7; Yaqui, 7; Zapotec, 7
 music, 13, 91, 144, 145, 167, 411, 575, 580, 702, 738; and art music,
  6, 12, 35, 73, 135, 289, 468, 827, 835; bibliography, 306, 320;
  Death Song, 371; European culture elements in, 130; folk music,
  145, 189, 289, 542, 643; in Indian schools, 180, 378, 804; in
  public schools, 308, 318, 731, 829; lullabies, 318, 745; record
  collections of, 64, 385; singing conventions of, 28; songs, 7, 41,
  106, 122, 124, 130, 165, 224, 233, 317, 402, 472, 548, 574, 634,

Jamaica, African music survivals, 272; folk music, 270
Japan, art music, 458; *bugaku*, 857; ceremonial music, 767; children's
    music, 523; early music, 194; foreign and national elements in
    music of, 295; *gagaku*, 246; *kabuki*, 803, 867; *kangen*, 301;
    music history, 20; music study in missionary schools of, 664;
    nagauta, 243, 506; *noh*, 409, 432, 587, 699; relationships of
    music with Okinawan classical songs, 442; *see also* Far East
Japanese, folksongs, 21; music aptitude and talent, 364, 475, 669
Jarabe tapatio, 157
Java, instruments, 569; *patet*, 334
Jazz, African elements in, 231, 292, 340, 360; analysis of, 631, 772, 808;
    and art music, 43, 73, 468, 630, 726, 770; and literature, 725;
    bibliography, 340; discography, 340; history, 808; improvisa-
    tion, 140; instruments, 530; Negro, 292, 474; New Orleans, 631;
    origins, 340; physiological effects of, 558; rhythm, 474; studies
    of musicians, 49, 751, 752; stylistic study, 710; swing, 121, 770;
    symphonic, 770; *see also* Blues; Dance bands
Jewish music, cantilation and accentuation, 737; folk music, 230; folksong,
    601; in Germany, 451; in U.S., 91; *see also* Hebrew music;
    Israel; Synagogue music
Jews, Babylonian, wedding songs, 138
Johnson, James Weldon, 153
Jota aragonesa, 97
Jubilees, Negro, 474, 652; *see also* Spirituals
Junior high schools, *see* Secondary schools

Kabuki, history and development, 803, 867
Kangen, music form of, 301
Kansas, folksongs, 862
Karnatic, *see* Carnatic
Kate, 132
Kavirondo, children's music, 663
Kentucky, ballads, 71; folk music, 114, 125; folksongs, 702
Keworkian, Komitas, Armenian folksongs collected by, 620
Kiltlied, 668
Kithara, 343
Knoxville, Tennessee, music history, 155
Kodály, Zoltán, 208
Kokonchomonshû, of N. Tachibana, as a source for Japanese music, 194
Korea, folksongs, 14, 401; instruments, 401; music, 390; music study in
    missionary schools, 664; *see also* Far East
Kriti, Carnatic, 31
Kulturkreise, and music, 345, 645
Kumanche Dance, Zuni Indians, 124

Labor songs, 220, 273
Laments, Corsica, 433; Provençale, 743
Langer, Susanne, and aesthetics of music, 66
Language and music, 870
Latin American music, 8, 133, 399, 513; African survivals in, 18, 154, 232,
    272, 360, 448, 531, 651, 822; children's songs, 801; Christmas
    carols, 592; folksongs, 414; in education, 316, 414; in works of
    L. M. Gottschalk, 185

Latvia, German folksongs in, 382
Layard Collection of recorded Malekulan music, 134
Legends, associated with dances in Mexico, 577
Libraries, public, popular sheet music in, 328
Linguistics and music, 680
Literature and music, 165, 179, 239, 252, 262, 309, 541, 547, 548, 559, 583, 602, 655, 693, 725, 735, 737, 766, 839
Lithuania, German folksongs in, 382
Lithuanians, music aptitude, 205
Loblied, 423
Lomax, John A. and Alan, and U.S. folksong tradition, 65
Lorraine, folksongs, 188, 742
Los Angeles, California, folk dance in, 455, 464
Louisiana, American Indian, British and Spanish influences on folk music of, 542; folksongs, 591, 642, 680, 787; French influences on music of, 542, 624, 680, 681; Negro music, 121, 185, 542, 579, 675, 787
Love songs, 98
Lü, in ancient China, 123, 661
Lullabies, North American Indian, 318, 745; Western Hemisphere, 239
Lumberjacks, songs and ballads, 46, 321, 444, 702
Lute, ancient Orient to medieval Europe, 521
Lutherans, church music, 722; hymnody, 855

Macedonia, *tupan* in, 19
Magyars, instruments, 38; songs, 420
Maharashtra, folk dances, 4
Maine, ballads and songs, 46, 355
Malekulan music, 134
Mallaca, music, 416
Mallorca, folksongs and dance, 42
Manny, Louise, Canadian ballad tunes collected by, 849
Manobo, ritual songs, 613
Manual for field workers, 261
Maori music, 496, 649
Maritime Provinces, folksongs, 355
Mask, significance in dance, 44
Masoretic music, 737
Mass media, and folksong revival, 603
Meaning in music, 66, 538, 633, 824
Measurement in music, 852; *see also* Ability, aptitude and talent studies
Medicine and music, 384; *see also* Therapy and music
Medicine Dance, 634
Melanesia, dance, 689; music, 285
Melodic sensitivity, of Negro and Caucasian children, 10
Melodies, ballads, 23, 79; composed by children, 765; Corsican laments, 433; folksongs, 22, 34, 249, 336, 352, 623, 672, 854; French, 69; *Nagauta*, 243; social songs, 291; *see also* Analysis
Mennonite church music, 864
Meter, 299, 424; antiquity, 252; Bulgarian folksongs, 83, 581; children's songs, 562
Methodist Episcopal church music, 323

Mexicans, dance in California, 392, 455; folksongs and dance in education, 369, 595; music talent, 116, 598
Mexico, children's songs, 801; dance, 7, 157, 284, 361, 367, 508, 577, 627; development of music, 786; folk music, 264, 367, 543, 556; folklore, 367; Indian music and dance, 7, 9, 35, 70, 130, 264, 281, 284, 317, 361, 367, 402, 508, 543, 634, 643, 688, 723, 842, 872; popular songs, 714; Spanish influences on music, 128; use of indigenous materials in art music, 35, 368, 543, 769
Middle Ages, German folksongs, 755; instruments of Turkestan, 351; traveling musicians, 676
Migrant workers, songs, 273
Military music, Austria, 593; Brandenburg, 646; Mormon, 628; sociological aspects of, 469
Miners' songs, Germany, 309; U.S., 273, 450
Minnesota music, sources and resources, 254
Minstrel show, U.S., 168
Miramichi Valley, ballads, 849
Mission music, California, 335
Missionary schools, music study in, 664
Mississippi, folksongs, 315, 344
Missouri, folksongs, 486, 591; rural children and music, 349
Modal practice, in Thai music, 557
Modality and folksong, 522
Modes, ancient Greece, 86; Coptic church, 55; ecclesiastical, 86; Hellenic music, 15; see also Tonal systems
Monongahela Valley, ballads, 78
Mood, relation to melodic pattern in folksong, 336
Moorish influence, on Hebrew music, 708; on Spanish music, 471, 657; on troubadours, 1
Moravian music, 91, 389, 482, 483
Mormon music, 191, 445, 480, 628, 720, 826
Moslems, influence on Spanish music, 471; music, 564
Mozarabic hymnal and chant, 11
Music drama based on American Indian music, 6
Music hall songs, 807
Music in the life of man, 653
Musical bow, South Africa, 115
Musicians, dance, 49; folk, 727; France, 588; Germany, 693, 817; in literary works, 693, 735; in Middle Ages, 676; jazz, 49, 751, 752; Negro, 51, 546, 811; patronage, 640; social status and development, 171, 381, 519, 588, 832; U.S., 49, 51, 381, 546, 727, 751, 752, 832
Musicians' associations, 226, 462, 467, 560, 685, 779; contracts, 322; Germany, 462, 560, 685, 779, 817; in antiquity, 226; in Middle Ages, 560
Mythology and music, 739; Greek, 719

Nagauta, 243, 506
Nägeli, Johann (Hans) Georg (1773-1836), 691
Nationalism and music, 35, 56, 73, 148, 230, 295, 468, 543, 556, 781
Nationality and ethnic group studies, 205, 245, 287, 364, 475, 852; see also Racial studies

139

Near East, instruments, 762

Negro music, 51, 60, 63, 73, 82, 91, 121, 142, 168, 173, 185, 207, 257, 272, 279, 306, 330, 337, 338, 360, 404, 474, 531, 602, 651, 663, 724, 780, 835; ability, aptitude and talent studies, 10, 61, 365, 598; Africa, 16, 53, 63, 82, 115, 142, 154, 173, 193, 207, 247, 272, 276, 279, 304, 311, 330, 337, 338, 360, 387, 404, 663, 724, 835, 840; and art music, 113, 153, 231, 251, 289, 358, 405, 546, 790, 792; dance, 63, 82, 387, 448; folk music, 113, 121, 145, 225, 251, 289, 315, 542, 580, 662, 702, 823, 848; folksongs, 65, 121, 159, 225, 255, 273, 315, 358, 395, 405, 444, 477, 546, 559, 579, 580, 675, 702, 787, 792, 793, 811, 837, 848; in education, 60, 61, 81, 118, 436, 604, 663, 759, 795, 845; instruments, 16, 53, 63, 82, 115, 193, 247, 276, 279, 304, 311, 530, 840; jazz, 231, 292, 340, 360, 468, 530, 631, 710, 725, 808; Latin America, 18, 154, 272, 360, 448, 531, 651, 780, 822; musicians, 51, 546; religious music, 162, 177, 395, 652, 721; spirituals, 121, 159, 225, 360, 456, 470, 525, 533, 591, 652, 785, 844; U.S., 10, 51, 60, 61, 65, 73, 81, 91, 113, 118, 121, 145, 153, 159, 162, 168, 177, 185, 225, 231, 251, 255, 257, 272, 273, 289, 292, 306, 315, 340, 358, 360, 365, 387, 395, 405, 436, 444, 456, 468, 470, 474, 477, 525, 530, 531, 533, 542, 546, 559, 579, 580, 591, 598, 602, 604, 631, 652, 662, 675, 702, 710, 721, 725, 759, 785, 787, 790, 792, 793, 795, 808, 811, 823, 837, 844, 845, 848

Netherlands, folk music and psalms, 101; songbook, 325; *see also* Holland

Neuhauss, Richard, collection of phonograph records of New Guinea music, 132

New Brunswick, ballads, 849

New Guinea, dance, 689; music, 132, 810

New Hebrides, Malekulan music, 134

New Mexico, dance, 8, 509; folksongs, 509, 771

New Orleans, jazz, 631

New York City, dance, 707

New Zealand, Maori music, 496, 649

Nigeria, music, 338

Noh drama, 409, 432, 587, 699

Nonliterate cultures, dance, 40, 147, 288, 293, 490, 648, 689, 835; instruments, 490; music, 52, 132, 210, 280, 285, 310, 345, 393, 416, 488, 547, 548, 613, 796, 835; *see also* Aboriginal music; Africa; Indians, American; Oceania

North America, ballads, 137, 321, 833; bibliographies of folklore, folksong, and Indian music, 306, 320; Indian lullabies, 745; music education in sixteenth and seventeenth centuries, 738

North Carolina, folk music, 54; singing conventions of Indians, 28

Northern Hemisphere, song and dance, 288

Norway, folk music, 258, 359, 749

Norwegians in U.S., folksongs, 183, 198, 639; music aptitude, 205

Notation, 312; character notes, 466; dance, 387, 711; for use by computers, 831; music of Coptic church, 55

Nova Scotia, ballads, 500

141

Protestants, church music, 859; psalms and hymns, 89, 747
Provençale, dance, 551; laments, 743
Prudentius, hymns of, 11
Prussia, folksong melodies, 672; military music, 646
Psalms and psalmody, Netherlands, 101; Presbyterians, 515; Protestants, 89, 747
Psychology and music, 13, 92, 209, 219, 278, 299, 313, 342, 422, 470, 511, 538, 571, 642, 682, 828, 859; *see also* Ability, aptitude and talent studies; Therapy and music
Puerto Rico, African survivals in, 154; folk music, 232
Puget Sound, dance, 841; folksongs, 413
Puritanism and music, 554
Pyrenees, folksongs, 383

Quodlibet, as source of folksong, 612

Racial studies, 116, 345, 517, 532, 598, 669, 852
Radio, influence on German music industry, 84
Raga, 213, 394, 516, 625
Railroad songs, 702
Recordings, archival collections, 64, 132, 134, 217, 385; influence on German music instrument industry, 84; miners' folksongs, 450; *see also* Discographies
Reformatories, songbooks, 791; *see also* Correctional institutions
Religion and dance, 40, 120, 149, 281, 723, 812
Religion and music, 204, 210, 453, 632, 719, 758, 827, 839, 859
Religious music, Armenia, 26, 174; Bulgaria, 667; Egypt and Ethiopia, 55; folksongs, 395, 716; Germany, 190, 690, 716; Holy Land Christians, 227; Hungary, 38; Scandinavia, 227, 573; Sweden, 108; U.S., 89, 91, 109, 143, 158, 159, 162, 177, 191, 225, 260, 281, 323, 327, 331, 335, 389, 395, 403, 445, 456, 468, 470, 474, 480, 482, 483, 494, 495, 515, 525, 533, 537, 550, 573, 591, 609, 628, 652, 677, 717, 720, 721, 722, 747, 785, 793, 811, 815, 826, 844, 855, 858, 864; *see also* Ceremonial music; Church music; Hymns and hymnody; Negro music; Psalms and psalmody
Revival music, 495
Revivals, folksong, 333, 603
Rhone, folksongs, 504
Rhythm, 424; African music, 337; antiquity, 252; ballads, 23; dance, 485, 734; folksongs, 83, 253, 262, 336, 581, 686, 757; in music, dance, and art, 734; Negro music, 474; *Noh* drama, 432; *see also* Analysis
River songs, 559, 836
Ritual dance, 508, 634, 812
Ritual music, American Indians, 13; Negro church, 162; New Hebrides, 134; Philippine Islands, 613; *see also* Ceremonial music
Role, of the American composer, 571
Role of music, ancient Greeks, 566; American Indians, 472, 872; non-literate cultures, 280; *see also* Function of music
Rome, ancient, music and instruments, 636; musicians' associations, 226; *see also* Antiquity
Ruanda, 279

142

Ruanda-Urundi, 82, 311
Rumania, folk music, 184; folksongs, 199, 656; funeral chants, 72; popular songs, 570
Rural children and music, 349
Russia, art music, 657, 700, 781; ballads, 152; church music, 326; dance, 753; early Byzantine music, 594; folksongs, 414, 700, 781; *see also* Soviet Union
Russians in U.S., music ability, 205

Sachs, Curt, *World History of the Dance* (1937), 147
Sacred dance, 812
Sacred music, Armenia, 26
Salzburgers in U.S., music, 91
Samoan music, 416
Satirical songs, 98, 355, 565
Savannah, Georgia, eighteenth century music in, 91
Scales, and aesthetic problems, 203; English folk music, 729; Iranian music, 39; pentatonic, 379, 788; *see also* Tonal systems
Scandinavians, folksongs, 302, 536; music ability, 245; music history, 605; religious music in U.S., 327, 573
Scarborough, Dorothy, folksong collections, 363, 793
Schools, American Indian, 180, 378, 804; American Indian music in, 829; Costa Rica, 873; El Salvador, 610; folk dance in, 369, 764, 809; folk festivals in, 512; folk music and songs in, 129, 167, 302, 332, 452, 764; Hawaiian, 744; Mormon, 720; music ability and talent studies, 61, 475, 598; Negro, 118, 845; Negro music in, 60, 81, 118, 845; teaching of improvisation in, 391; U.S., 60, 61, 81, 118, 129, 167, 180, 302, 332, 369, 378, 391, 452, 475, 512, 598, 720, 764, 804, 809, 829, 845; *see also* Colleges and universities; Elementary schools; Secondary schools
Scottish, dance, 387; music in U.S., 91
Scottish ballads, bibliography, 493; Christian elements in, 833; Denmark, 535; love, 596; North America, 833; Nova Scotia, 500; popular, 100; social criticism in, 706; text and melody in, 79; tune variants, 339; U.S., 99, 100, 265; *see also* British
Seashore, Carl E., music talent tests, 116, 287, 364, 365, 615, 834
Secondary schools, American Indian music, 731; dance, 846; folk music and songs, 183, 307, 316, 350, 376, 555, 595, 777, 778, 795; music ability and achievement studies, 205, 237, 364, 599; Negro music, 759, 795; *see also* Schools
Semitic music, 481; *see also* Hebrew music; Jewish music
Senfl, Ludwig, 670
Serbia, funeral chants, 72; wedding songs, 421
Serbo-Croatians, folk music, 184, 240
Shakers, music, 143
Shamanism and music, 758
Sharagan, 26
Sharp, Cecil, *English Folk Songs from the Southern Appalachians* (1932), 339
Sialum, 132
Singing conventions, North Carolina Indians, 28

143

Singing games, European, 324; Tennessee, 267; *see also* Play-party songs and dance
Siwah Oasis (U.A.R.), music, 687
Slave songs, U.S., 225; *see also* Spirituals
Slavonic chant, Byzantine elements in, 805
Slavs, music ability and talent, 205, 245
Slovakia, folk music, 184
Slovenia, folk music and songs, 129, 601; instruments, 90
Smetana, Bedrich F., 697
Social psychology and music, 13, 511, 571
Social songs, 291, 617
Socially maladjusted, effects of music on, 278
Societies, German-American in California, 182; musicians in Germany, 560; music, 750
Society Islands, dance, 147
Sociology and music, 4, 40, 49, 127, 134, 162, 166, 171, 192, 212, 277, 280, 380, 381, 453, 469, 489, 495, 498, 519, 541, 588, 599, 603, 616, 638, 673, 696, 706, 750, 751, 752, 779, 796, 797, 798, 817, 832, 839
Songbooks, Antwerp, 325; bibliography, 58; popular, 602; reformatory schools, 791
Songs, Afro-Bahian cults, 531; American Indians, 7, 41, 106, 122, 124, 130, 165, 224, 233, 317, 371, 402, 470, 472, 545, 548, 574, 634, 732, 816, 829, 842, 847; ancient Egypt, 457; ancient Greece, 111; Andalusian Gypsies, 633; Antwerp, 325; Assyrian, 578; Australian Aborigines, 561; Bulgarian, 422, 606, 667; Bulu, 404; campaign, 17; chansons, 681, 802, 869; Chinese, 45; choral, 111; Civil War, U.S., 96, 858; collections, 80, 477; Creole, 121, 185, 579, 675; democracy in, 426; England, 80, 478; epic, 422, 606; Eskimo, 167, 490, 510; Florida, 501; Forty-Niners, 268; Germany, 423, 524, 668, 698, 814; Hanoverian Succession, 478; Hawaiian, 778, 798; India, 31, 217, 679; jazz, 474; Jews, 138; *kiltlied*, 668; laments, 433, 743; *loblied*, 423; Magyars, 420; Maori, 649; melodic-harmonic relationships, 291; music hall, 807; nonliterate peoples, 132, 547, 548; Northern Hemisphere, 288; Okinawa, 442; peasant, 421, 611; plantation, 579; play-party, 77, 163, 591; Polish, 435; revival, 495; satirical, 98, 355, 565; Serbian, 421; social, 291, 617; soldier, 698; *tagelied*, 524; Tlingit, 510; U.S., 17, 41, 67, 71, 77, 96, 98, 106, 121, 122, 124, 127, 150, 163, 165, 185, 212, 224, 233, 268, 288, 315, 317, 328, 355, 371, 380, 402, 426, 449, 472, 474, 491, 494, 495, 501, 515, 545, 548, 559, 565, 574, 576, 579, 591, 634, 652, 675, 681, 702, 714, 732, 783, 816, 829, 842, 847, 858; war, 96, 315, 449, 559, 576, 698, 797, 858; wedding, 138, 421; *see also* Carols; Children's songs; Gospel songs; Popular songs
Songsters, U.S., 176, 454, 784
Songwriters, 212; *see also* Composers
Souterliedekens, 101
South Africa, children's songs, 63; musical bow, 115; music, 142, 207
South America, instruments, 356; music, 133
Soviet culture, attitude toward music, 215
Soviet Union, composers and political ideology, 202; *see also* Russia

144

Spain, dance, 248; folksongs, 97; instruments, 821; music, 471, 633, 657
Spanish, ballads and folk music, 8, 35, 91, 148, 204, 232, 315, 501, 502,
509, 542, 771; dance, 8, 392, 509, 592; in Latin America, 35,
128, 148, 502; in North America, 738; in U.S., 8, 91, 315, 392,
501, 509, 542, 592, 771; music ability, capacity and achieve-
ment, 237, 475; national hymns, 148
Spirituals, 73; African influence on, 360; Caucasian, 158, 260, 537, 844;
Negro, 121, 159, 225, 456, 470, 525, 533, 591, 652, 785, 844;
see also Jubilees
Stravinsky, Igor, 113
Strophic development, of folksongs, 619
Sturm und Drang period, folksongs, 406
Style, 856; American Indian music, 574, 575, 872; blues, 710; German
music, 638; Okinawan vocal, 442; Rumanian popular song, 570;
see also Analysis
Sudanic languages, terms for instruments in, 304
Sükrüllah, Ahmedoglu, and Turkish instruments, 234
Sumerian culture, music, 300
Sun Dance, American Indian, 372, 695, 741, 766, 806
Swabia, folk dance, 641; folksongs, 415, 683
Sweden, religious music, 108
Swedish in U.S., dance, 464, 764; folk music, 601, 764; music aptitude,
205; sacred and secular music, 573
Swing, 121, 770
Switzerland, music in elementary schools, 591
Symphony orchestra, social organization of, 832
Synagogue music, 187, 269, 507, 690, 708; see also Hebrew music; Jewish
music
Syncopation, 424
Syria, hymns, 172

Tabla, 760
Tachibana, Narisue, *Kokonchomonshû,* 194
Tagelied, 524
Tala, 213, 394, 586
Talent, *see* Ability, aptitude and talent
Tam-man Nacup, 293
Tampa, Florida, Spanish songs and ballads in, 501
Tanganyika, dance, instruments and music, 82
Taosug, music, 796
Taste in music, 179, 209, 323, 696; *see also* Aesthetics and music
Tennessee, folk music, 155, 242
Terminology, instruments in Sudanic languages, 304; U.S. country dances,
170; used by Plato, 15
Texas, folk music, 850; folksongs, 107, 141, 591; music in Negro schools,
759, 795
Textile workers, folksongs, 273
Texts, American Indian songs, 41, 224, 233, 293, 317, 470, 545, 548, 574;
Bagobo, 52; Bulgarian folksongs, 757; Canadian folksongs, 167,
499; chansons of Louisiana, 681; chanteys, 117; Chinese songs,
45; French songs, 94; English and Scottish ballads, 79, 80, 99,
339, 540; English folksongs, 141, 333; Eskimo songs, 490; Euro-

145

pean folksongs in Illinois, 601; "Frankie and Albert," 105; German folksongs, 333; gospel songs, 260; lullabies, 239; Mexican *corrido*, 367; Negro folksongs, 477; Norwegian folksongs in U.S., 198; Okinawan classical songs, 442; Peyote songs, 479; play-party songs, 77; Polish folksongs in Detroit, 607; popular songs, 94, 127; songs of India, 217; songs of nonliterate peoples, 52, 547, 548; Turkish folksongs, 179, 196; U.S. ballads and folksongs, 76, 77, 80, 87, 99, 105, 117, 127, 141, 151, 198, 260, 339, 344, 444, 449, 477, 486, 492, 541, 559, 601, 681, 768, 836; Venda children's songs, 63; war songs, 449; *see also* Poetry and music

Thailand, music, 557
Theater and music, *see* Drama and music
Theory, music, of India, 568; of China, 860
Therapy and music, 68, 193, 278, 294, 297, 427, 621, 733; *see also* Psychology and music
Thrace, folksongs, 623
Thuringia, folksongs, 692
Tiberian music, 737
Tiv, music, 338
Tonal systems, China, 430; Turkish classical music, 197
Tonality, Bulgarian folksongs, 623; Japanese folksongs, 21; *see also* Analysis
Traits, of Negro song, 477
Transcription, and electronic computer, 589
Travelers' accounts, references to music and dance in, 142, 147, 547, 835
Trinidad, African patterns in Negro music, 822
Troubadours, Arabian influences, 1; influence on Hebrew music, 708; instruments, 274
Tune-books, bibliography, 89, 206, 466
Tunes, folk ballads and songs, 76, 77, 78; *see also* Melodies
Tunisia, music, 434
Tupan, Macedonia, 19
Turkestan, instruments, 351
Turkey, folksongs, 179; instruments, 234; tonality of classical music, 197
Turkish music, in art music, 184, 835
Turks, Ottoman, urban music, 196

Uganda, dance, instruments and music, 82
Uhland, Ludwig, *Alte hoch- und niederdeutsche Volkslieder* (1844), 524
Ukrainia, folk music, 184
UNESCO, and intercultural music education, 654
Ungoni, music, 329
Union of Soviet Socialist Republics, *see* Russia; Soviet Union
United States, ability, aptitude and talent studies, 205, 237, 245, 354, 365, 475, 517, 532, 598, 599, 669, 680, 709, 833, 834; art music, 6, 12, 43, 73, 113, 135, 153, 185, 198, 202, 251, 358, 396, 405, 468, 546, 558, 571, 614, 726, 746, 790, 792, 832; contributions of foreign cultures, 8, 14, 32, 59, 91, 99, 100, 129, 137, 141, 150, 167, 182, 183, 198, 254, 262, 265, 296, 302, 306, 327, 344, 348, 350, 369, 387, 392, 452, 455, 464, 482, 483, 487, 501, 509, 512, 539, 542, 573, 578, 580, 595, 601, 607, 614, 624, 764, 798,

799, 809, 820; dance, 8, 25, 73, 77, 146, 155, 170, 175, 238, 290, 296, 305, 369, 370, 387, 392, 455, 464, 509, 585, 658, 707, 734, 764, 809, 846; folk ballads, lore, music and songs, 8, 17, 23, 30, 32, 37, 46, 54, 59, 65, 71, 73, 76, 77, 78, 87, 96, 98, 99, 100, 103, 105, 107, 114, 121, 125, 129, 137, 141, 143, 145, 150, 151, 156, 163, 167, 183, 185, 198, 225, 242, 251, 255, 261, 262, 265, 267, 268, 273, 289, 291, 302, 306, 307, 315, 319, 321, 332, 336, 339, 344, 348, 350, 355, 358, 363, 396, 414, 444, 450, 452, 468, 474, 477, 486, 492, 501, 509, 512, 539, 541, 542, 549, 553, 555, 559, 572, 578, 579, 580, 591, 595, 601, 603, 607, 614, 624, 628, 629, 639, 654, 662, 675, 680, 681, 682, 702, 707, 720, 726, 727, 746, 764, 768, 771, 777, 787, 792, 793, 811, 820, 823, 831, 833, 836, 837, 843, 844, 848, 850, 862; Indian music and dance, 6, 12, 13, 28, 33, 41, 62, 64, 70, 73, 91, 92, 95, 106, 122, 124, 135, 136, 139, 144, 145, 165, 169, 180, 189, 218, 224, 233, 241, 250, 254, 277, 281, 289, 293, 306, 308, 315, 317, 318, 320, 335, 354, 357, 371, 372, 378, 385, 400, 402, 411, 413, 460, 468, 472, 473, 479, 514, 542, 545, 548, 567, 574, 575, 580, 634, 660, 669, 688, 695, 702, 705, 709, 715, 723, 728, 731, 732, 739, 741, 745, 766, 774, 800, 804, 806, 816, 827, 829, 834, 841, 842, 847, 850, 853, 866; Negro music, 10, 51, 60, 61, 65, 81, 91, 113, 118, 121, 145, 153, 159, 162, 168, 177, 185, 225, 231, 251, 255, 257, 272, 273, 289, 292, 315, 340, 358, 360, 365, 387, 395, 405, 436, 444, 456, 470, 474, 477, 525, 531, 533, 542, 546, 559, 579, 580, 591, 598, 602, 604, 631, 652, 662, 702, 721, 759, 785, 787, 790, 792, 793, 795, 811, 823, 837, 844, 845, 848; other music references, 43, 49, 51, 67, 71, 73, 91, 105, 127, 140, 150, 155, 168, 176, 182, 206, 209, 212, 229, 231, 233, 254, 257, 272, 292, 328, 335, 340, 349, 360, 366, 380, 381, 426, 449, 454, 465, 466, 468, 469, 491, 530, 546, 554, 558, 565, 573, 595, 628, 630, 631, 682, 696, 702, 710, 714, 720, 725, 726, 727, 734, 751, 752, 772, 783, 784, 797, 808, 811, 832

Vadé, Jean-Joseph (1719-1757), and vaudeville, 563
Variants, ballads, 23, 78, 87, 100, 105, 137, 141, 339, 444, 549, 596; folksongs, 499, 639, 851
Variations, folksongs, 78, 437
Vaudeville, 459, 563
Vaughan Williams, Ralph, 56, 522, 608
Vedic music, 217
Venda, music, 63
Vermont, early music, 229
Vienna Phonogramm-Archiv, 217
Vikings, music, 749
Virgin Islands, music, 439
Virginia, folksongs, 141
Visual arts and music, 660, 734
Vocal style and techniques, Pueblo and Pima Indians, 317; Okinawan classical songs, 442

War songs, German, 698; U.S., 96, 315, 449, 559, 576, 858
Wars and music, 51, 682, 797

147